Selected Quality Metrics for Digital Passport Photographs

Vom Fachbereich Informatik
der Technischen Universität Darmstadt
genehmigte

Dissertation

Zur Erlangung des akademischen Grades
Doktor-Ingenieurs (Dr.-Ing.)

von
Oriana Yuridia González Castillo
aus Cuernavaca, Morelos
Mexiko

Referenten der Arbeit:
Prof. Dr. José L. Encarnação, Technische Universität Darmstadt
Prof. Dr. Stephen Wolthusen, Royal Holloway University of London

Tag der Einreichung: 26.10.2007
Tag der mündliche Prüfung: 12.12.2007
Hochschulkennziffer D17

Bibliografische Information der Deutschen Nationalbibliothek

Die Deutsche Nationalbibliothek verzeichnet diese Publikation in der
Deutschen Nationalbibliografie; detaillierte bibliografische Daten sind
im Internet über http://dnb.d-nb.de abrufbar.

ISBN 978-3-8325-1965-0

Gedruckt mit freundlicher Unterstützung des DAAD.

Logos Verlag Berlin GmbH
Comeniushof, Gubener Str. 47,
10243 Berlin
Tel.: +49 030 42 85 10 90
Fax: +49 030 42 85 10 92
INTERNET: http://www.logos-verlag.de

Acknowledgements

This work was developed thanks to the facilities provided by the Fraunhofer-Institute for Computer Graphics Darmstadt (Fraunhofer IGD), the founds provided for the Consejo Nacional de Ciencia y Tecnología (CONACyT) México and the Deutscher Akademischer Austausch Dienst (DAAD) Germany.

The development of this thesis in Germany has been one of the best experiences in my life. I learned many things which I could not have learned in any other country. This thesis represents the culmination of the biggest dream I ever had. I want to thank all the people who supported me to make it possible: Stephanie Buechl, Dr. Volker Roth, Dr. Christoph Busch, Prof. José L. Encarnação, Dr. Stephen Wolthusen, Dr. Martin Schmucker, Dr. Henning Daum, Dr. Ullrich Pinsdorf, Dipl. Ing. Alexander Nouak and all the colleagues of the department A8 from Fraunhofer IGD in Darmstadt. I also want to thank to: Elfriede Fitschen, Elke Frank, Sabine Bartsch, Doris Müller, Barbara Merten, Carola Eichel and my friends Ana, Adriana, Francisco, Chetna, Sebastian, Jaime, Sonja, Mariza, Erica, Roberto C., Kresimir Delac, Raúl Aguirre, and the people who collaborate in the development of the software to implement the methodologies developed: Juan Guerrero, Qi Han, Mathias Frohna, Gülnur Derelioglu and Alexander Alexandrov.

My family in Mexico has played a very important role in the development of my career. Thanks for the unconditional support of my parents and brothers. I am very grateful with my husband and his family who have motivated me and supported me with all the corrections. I want to mention my special thanks to Armin Neuss, Jürgen Jannik, to my friends from the KHG Darmstadt and to the Prof. José L. Encarnação for his support during the development of this thesis.

Thanks to all the people who made this dream possible.

Oriana Yuridia González Castillo
Darmstadt, 26th October 2007,

Abstract

Facial images play a significant role as biometric identifier. The accurate identification of individuals is nowadays becoming more and more important and can have a big impact on security. The good quality of facial images in passport photographs is essential for accurate identification of individuals. The quality acceptance procedure presently used is based on human visual perception and thus subjective and not standardized. Existing algorithms for measuring image quality are applied for all types of images not focused on the quality determination of passport photographs. However there are few documents existing, defining conformance requirements for the determination of digital passport photographs quality. A major document is named "Biometrics Deployment of Machine Readable Travel Documents", published by the International Civil Aviation Organization (ICAO).

This thesis deals with the development of metrics for the automated determination of the quality and grade of acceptance of digital passport photographs without having any reference image available. Based on the above mentioned document of the ICAO, quality conformance sentences and related attributes are abstracted with self-developed methods. About fifty passport photographs haven been taken under strictly controlled conditions to fulfill all requirements given by the above mentioned document. Different kinds of algorithms were implemented to determine values for image attributes and to detect the face features. This ground truth database was the source to "translate" natural language into numeric values to describe how "good quality" is represented by numbers.

No priority for the evaluation of attributes was given in the ICAO document. For that reason an international online and on-site survey was developed to explore the opinion of user experts whose work is related to passport photographs. They were asked to evaluate the relevance of different types of attributes related to a passport photograph. Based on that survey, weights for the different types of attributes have been calculated. These weights express the different importances of the attributes for the evaluation process. Three different metrics, expressed by the Photograph-/Image-/Biometric Attributes-Quality Indexes (PAQI, IAQI, BAQI) have been developed to obtain reference values for the quality determination of a passport photograph.

Another metric developed is called "Non-Conformance Quality Index" which is based on the representation of the quality information in the minimum unit of information storage: the byte. The nonconformance of a quality attribute is stored in a bit. For a digital passport photograph the representation of the quality attributes is defined by four bytes. Every byte has eight bits and every bit represents an attribute.

Experiments are described to show, that the quality of a selected digital passport photograph can be measured and different attributes, which have an impact on the quality and on the recognition of face features can be identified. Critical issues are discussed and the thesis closes with recommendations given for further research approaches.

Zusammenfassung

Passbilder spielen eine wichtige Rolle bei der Identifizierung von Personen. Da die Personenerkennung gegenwärtig immer mehr an Bedeutung gewinnt und die Genauigkeit der Erkennung einen großen Einfluß auf verschiedene Sicherheitsaspekte haben kann, ist die gute Qualität von Passbildern unerläßlich. Gegenwärtig erfolgt die Bestimmung der Qualität durch Personen. I ist daher geprägt von der persönlichen Wahrnehmung und unterliegt damit subjektiven und nicht standardisierten Kriterien. Zwar existieren bereits Algorithmen, die zur automatischen Qualitätsbestimmung digitaler Fotos benutzt werden, diese sind aber nicht speziell auf Passbilder abgestimmt. Das bedeutsamste Dokument, das sich mit der Definition von Kriterien zur Bestimmung der Qualität digitaler Passbilder beschäftigt trägt den Titel "Biometrics deployment of machine readable travel documents" und wurde von der International Civil Aviation Organization (ICAO) veröffentlicht.

Diese Dissertation beschreibt die Entwicklung von Metriken, um die Qualität von digitalen Paßbildern automatisiert und objektiv ohne den Zugriff auf ein Referenzbild zu bestimmen. Basierend auf dem o.g. Dokument der ICAO wurden die Qualitätskriterien und -attribute nach einer selbst entwickelten Methodik zusammengefasst. Etwa fünfzig Passbilder sind digital unter exakt kontrollierten Bedingungen aufgenommen worden, so dass Sie alle Anforderungen aus dem o.g. Dokument erfüllen. Diese Datenbank dient als Basis, um die schriftlich formulierten Anforderungen in Zahlenwerte zu "übersetzen" und die Darstellung von "guter Qualität" in Zahlenform zu ermöglichen. Die Werte für die Attribute wurden durch den Einsatz verschiedener Algorithmen ermittelt. Da durch das Dokument der ICAO keine Rangfolge der Attribute vorgenommen wird, wurde eine internationale Online- und vor-Ort-Befragung durchgeführt um die Meinung von Experten, die in Ihrem Beruf sehr viel mit Passbildern zu tun haben, zu erfragen. Sie wurden u.a. gebeten eine Priorisierung der verschiedenen Attribute vorzunehmen. Basierend auf diesen Angaben wurden Gewichtungen berechnet. Drei Metriken wurden entwickelt, um Referenzwerte zur Qualitätsbestimmung zu erhalten: Photograph-/Image-/Biometric Attributes-Quality Indexes (PAQI, IAQI, BAQI).

Es wurden Experimente durchgeführt, um zu zeigen, dass die Qualität von Passbildern gemessen werden kann und dass einzelne Attribute, die zur Gesichtserkennung notwendig sind und gewisse Qualitätsanforderungen nicht erfüllen, identifiziert werden können. Die Arbeit schließt mit einer Diskussion kritischer Aspekte und Empfehlungen für weitere Forschungsansätze.

Contents

List of Tables

v

List of Figures

Chapter 1

Introduction

1.1 Motivation

Since the European Commission adopted the face image as a mandatory biometric identifier for passports, face images have been playing a significant role as biometric sample in several studies to assess the quality of personal identification documents. The purpose of biometric documents is to limit the use of fraudulent documents by achieving a more accurate authentication of individuals. The passport photograph quality acceptance procedure presently used is based on the human visual perception which is subjective and has no standardization. The quality of an image can be automatically calculated by different algorithms. However the existing algorithms for measuring the image quality are applied for all types of images, not specially for face images.

1.2 Research Objective

Objective of this work is the development of metrics to automatically determine the quality and grade of acceptance of digital passport photographs without having any reference image. The metrics are based on the abstraction of the quality conformance requirements of the Machine Readable Travel Documents (MRTD) document from the International Civil Aviation Organization (ICAO) ICAO/MRTD[48] and based on the document of the International Standardization Organization called Biometric Data Interchange Formats Part Five for Face Image Data (ISO/IEC 19794-5)[4].

1.3 Structure of the Thesis

The relevance of the topic is described in Chapter 2. Chapter 3 deals with the theoretical background; the essential terms like quality, biometrics and image quality are examined. In Chapter 4 the Quality Conformance sentences are analyzed by considering the documents[48] and [4]. After the analysis, the requirements are categorized; for that purpose a self-developed on-line and on-site international survey has been conducted with participants, whose work is deeply related with facial images. The methodology and results of the international survey are detailed in Chapter 5. This survey found remarkable acceptance as a pioneer work to share the results and the methodology with the scientifical community, the results have already been published under: `http://www.face-rec.org/interestingpapers/ Standards/2dfiqsurveyreport_OYGC.pdf`

Chapter 6 describes the experimentation phase and how the reference values for Image Quality Attributes can be determined. As in this thesis the approach for determining Facial Image Quality is based on the extraction of values for Image Quality Attributes and for Biometric Quality Attributes, Chapter 7 describes the methods and algorithms implemented to detect face features and to define the reference values for Biometric Quality Attributes. In Chapter 8 the new knowledge gets combined to describe the creation and implementation of series of formulas to calculate conventional quality indexes and a non-conformance quality index for a digital passport photograph. Chapter 9 presents a summary of contributions, discussion of results and recommendations for future research.

Chapter 2

Relevance of the Research Objective

2.1 Background of Personal Identification Documents

Individuals can be identified by three basic means: by something they have knowledge of (password or secret code), something in their possession (a card or key), or something that reflects a unique feature (physical or physiological characteristics). These characteristic groups are the fundamentals of biometrics. The term "biometrics" is derived from the Greek words "bio" (life) and "metrics" (to measure). Automated biometric systems have only become available over the last few decades due to significant advances in the field of computer processing. Many of these new automated techniques, however, are based on ideas that were originally conceived hundreds, even thousands of years ago. [49]

The condition of having an identification document established permits the individual to present its personal identity. In order to have the desired degree of trust in the identification process it contains as minimum requirements name and photo. Examples for official personal identification documents are: passport, visa, driver's license, personal identity card, health insurance certificate, citizenship's card, school or university identity card.

2.1.1 Passport

In this section an overview of passports' description and the history of the evolution of passports are given. As examples used are the United Kingdom's passport and the German electronic passport. A passport is an official government document that certifies one's identity and citizenship. It permits a citizen to travel to a foreign country allowing one to transport goods or to travel through that country; adapted from [9]. Passport specifications went through changes over and over again through the time. The first modern passport in United Kingdom (UK) [60] was made of one page folded into eight with a card cover. The holder information contained was the personal information such as description, occupation, country of residence, distinguishing marks and height. It also included person's shape of face, features (nose: large, forehead: broad, eyes: small), complexion and color of eyes. the first modern passport also contained a holder's semi frontal photo in black and white and as security measure it included the holder's signature. The validity was expressed in series of four two years periods. The passport's variations for families were the introduction of a book-form with thirty two pages.

The first two pages contained the family information and a description with frontal photo in black and white showing the family members. Figure 2.1 shows an example of the modern passport issued in the United Kingdom in 1915.

Figure 2.1: Example of Modern Passport from United Kingdom of 1915

The first generation of UK's modern passports contained a glued holder's semi frontal photo in black and white, the specification of personal holder's characteristics was also included. Table 2.1 represents a summary of the specifications established in UK for the first generation of modern passports. The registered second generation of the UK's modern passports dates back to 1972 and 1973. Table 2.2 describes the most relevant changes implemented, for example the book-form with 30 and 94 pages respectively, the validity period and important security features. In 1981 a further security feature was added to the laminate by incorporating a security laminate overprint. The next generations of UK's passports included some minor changes such as the reduction in numbers of pages and the inclusion of security paper incorporating a special water-mark. At the end of the 1980s some countries started the initiative to use Machine Readable Passports (MRP). The main characteristics implemented are described in Table 2.3. In 1998 the International Civil Aviation Organization (ICAO) and the Council of Members of the European Community implemented as additional security feature the transfer of the holder's personal data from the inside of the back cover to the passport's last page. A digitally printed face image of the holder (instead of a glued in photograph) is used. The specification of the detailed "vision of the future" of security features for the UK's passport is presented in Table 2.4.

On 28th February of 2005 the European Commission adopted the first part of the technical specifications for biometric passports which calls for the storage of the face image of the holder on a contactless chip in the passport. The protection of this image is ensured by "Basic Access Control" which requires reading the machine-readable zone in the passport for opening the chip. This commission decision triggered the implementation time frame, so that all member states have to implement the face image requirements on passports at the latest on 28th August 2006. As a consequence all member states will also fulfill the US requirements for the visa waiver countries to issue biometrically enabled passports by October 2006.

On 28th of June 2006 the second part of the technical specifications, required for the introduction of biometric identifiers (fingerprints) into the passport and other travel documents was issued by the member states following Council Regulation (EC) 2252/2004 [8]. On 1st November 2005 the Federal Republic of Germany was one of the first countries in the European Union to introduce the electronic passport with biometric data (called ePass).

Presently the chip integrated into the ePass stores the usual passport data, the passport photograph and also includes two digital fingerprints. In the next few years, not only the Member States of the EU, but also Japan, the United States, Australia, Russia, Canada, Switzerland and others will introduce passports with an electronic biometric function, this ePass is called biometric passport.

A biometric passport is a combined paper and electronic identity document that uses biometrics to authenticate the citizenship of travelers. The passport's critical information is stored on a tiny Radio Frequency IDentification (RFID) computer chip, similar to information stored on smart cards. Like some smart cards, the passport book design calls for an embedded contactless chip that is able to hold digital signature data to ensure the integrity of the passport and the biometric data. Figure 2.2 shows the latest passport developed in Germany. The special characteristics of this electronic passport are related to security features. Most of them are physical characteristics such as the laminated protective layer that protects the data page and the contactless chip as well as the module integrated into the passport's cover. The data page of the German passport contains most of the security features of the passport. Figure 2.3 shows the details of these features. The first seven elements compound the group of new security symbols called Identigram, designed for the Bundesdruckerei [16]. Table 2.5 describes every security feature included, the first seven features are the Identigram's elements.

Considering the UK's modern passport and the electronic German passport as representative examples, the difference between both examples is defined by the technology used and the implementation of security features. The ePass contains an integrated computer chip that is capable of storing information from the data page which contains a photo (in JPEG2000 format), name, sex, date of birth, passport number, nationality, issuer, expiring date, digital fingerprint and more. These changes allow a better appreciation of the evolution of the passport as personal identity document in the last century.

2.1.2   Driver's License

The driver's license has been considered in some countries as an official personal identity document; it is an official document which specifies in detail if a person has the necessary qualifications to operate a motorized vehicle. There are some restrictions for obtaining the driver's license. The applicable specifications vary depending on the issuing country and the type of driver's license. The first general restriction concerns the driving test, i.e. different parts: namely praxis and theory. Another restriction is the driver's age. In most countries

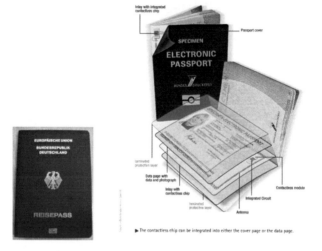

Figure 2.2: German Electronic Passport in 2005

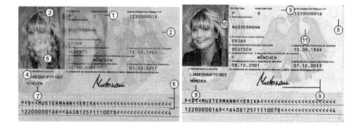

Figure 2.3: Security Features of the German Electronic Passport

the permitted age for driving a car or van is 17 years. Obtaining a provisional license at the age of 16 years is also possible. Since the standardization took place in 1998, all EU country members issue licenses in a standard format, regardless of the language of the license holder [31]. A holder of a license from any EU member country is allowed to drive in any other EU country.

However, this document is not valid for ID use. In most of the European countries an ID card with photo is required in addition to the driver's license and both must be presented whenever requested. In some countries such as USA and Canada, the driver's license serves as the primary means of photo identification and proof of age. It is often used as the facto equivalent for completion of many transactions. The current driver's license by the EU includes the following holder's information: a photograph of the bearer, family name, first name(s), date and place of birth, issue date, expiry date of the license, issued by, license number, signature of bearer, valid categories, issue date of the category, expiry date of the category, restrictions (number coded).

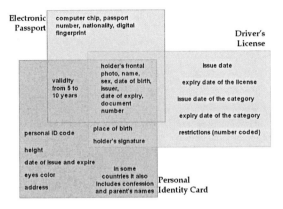

Figure 2.4: Common Features between Personal Identity Documents

2.1.3 Personal Identity Card

The Personal Identity Card is issued by the state. It was created to certify the identity of the bearer. Several countries issue an official national identity card that allows business and governmental transactions. The use of the national identity cards varies depending on the country, for example for some European countries it may be used as proof of identity and it may be used instead of a passport to travel within 32 European countries. In most of the countries it is also valid in terms of complying with legal requirements such as passport applications, to fight tax evasion, opening a bank account, get admission to an university, local census, tax purposes, marriage and firearms licenses. In some other countries the national identity document is the electoral card and it is used as a proof of citizenship. The holder's information included on a traditional identity card covers the card number, personal ID code, face image, nationality, first and last names, gender, date of birth, issuing authority, eye color, height, place of birth, signature, date of issue and expiry and address. In some countries it also includes passport number, confession and parent's names. The validity of the identity card in most of the countries ranges from 5 to 10 years. Some of the countries having such a compulsory identity card are Mexico, Argentina, Brazil, Chile, Hong Kong, Belgium, Germany, Greece, Luxemburg, Indonesia, Israel, Malaysia, Romania, Singapore, Croatia, Egypt, Thailand, Spain, Cyprus, Czech Republic, Estonia, Malta, Poland, Slovakia and Bulgaria. Other countries having such a voluntary identity card are Austria, Finland, France, Italy, Netherlands, Portugal, Sweden and Slovenia. The countries that do not issue such an identity card are Denmark, Ireland,

USA, Australia, Canada, Iceland, Latvia and Lithuania. In recent years identity cards have evolved and have gained more importance around the world.

Some international joint efforts to standardize the card specifications are already in process. An example [25] is an international standard, which describes the card's characteristics and provides criteria to which cards shall conform. It specifies the requirements for such cards used for international interchange. This standard specifies the physical characteristics such as size and dimensions of the card, bending stiffness, adhesion or blocking, resistance to heat, surface distortions and contamination. It also refers to the construction and materials of the identification cards.

Identity cards serve as a basis to the governmental system in its intent to control the existence and movements of citizens by means of registration. However, this system found opponents in the US and in Canada who argued that such ID cards might easily be misused as an instrument of an annoying observation by the state.
In recent years initiatives to introduce a Europe-wide biometric ID card have taken priority for the EU Commission. In July 2005 the Presidency of the Council of the European Union sent a document [5] to the Strategic Committee on Immigration, Frontiers and Asylum demanding taking into account the achievements in relation to the use of biometrics, common standards for the card interface, measures (including Enhanced Access Control and PKI) which may be used to ensure that data stored on Identity Cards is appropriately protected but can be read by other member states. The first draft of conclusions was required by end of March 2006.

2.2   Automatization of Face Images Quality Determination

A personal identity document contains the set of behavioral or personal characteristics by which an individual is recognizable as member of a group [9]. Before the computer gained such a high influence on the issuing and authorization process of personal identity documents this process was divided into four main phases: application, registering, approval and use. Figure 2.5 shows the first general scheme of this process. In the first phase individuals are requested to personally present the original documents for proof of name and date of birth. Generally the document requested is the birth certificate. An impressed photo in black and white is also required. The registering organization gathers individual's information and registers it in its archives before an identity number is assigned. The personal identity document was previously printed and it was completed manually or by using a typewriter, one photo in black and white was adhered manually in the document and another photo was adhered in the archive book. To warrant the authenticity of a personal identity document it was sealed around the photo. In the use of the personal identity document the authentication was implicit. Third organizations trusted in the individual presenting the identity seeing it's photograph and if the owner and the identity matched they were sufficient proves for accepting the identification. Traditionally, the process for the issue of personal identification documents was based on paper books archives to register the individual's information. Individuals trusting was guaranteed for the organization of registering. Originality and validity of a personal identity document was implicit on its use. In this process, mechanical typewriters and telephones were the

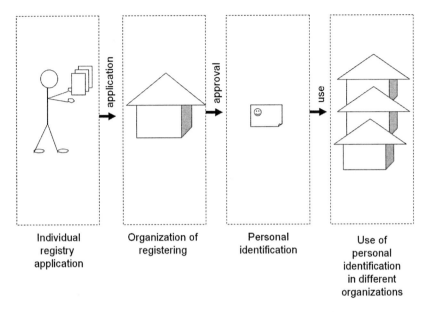

| Individual registry application | Organization of registering | Personal identification | Use of personal identification in different organizations |

Figure 2.5: Earliest Age of the Process for the Issue of Personal Identity Documents

main work tools, the main human resources in the registering offices were the secretaries and archivists who were specialized people in information management. Process for the issue of personal identity documents had its first evolution with the integration of the authentication phase: a copy of register archives was distributed within third organizations to validate the register or authorization of an individual. In Figure 2.6 the variation in the process can be appreciated through the second scheme of personal identity process.

2.2.1 Process for the Issue of Personal Identity Documents During First Computer Revolution

The human societies experienced several changes in the 1980's. The introduction of desktop computers in offices lead to consequent changes. Some changes related to the experience of office technology growth had their influence on the mechanization of tasks, automation of data processing, proliferation and organization of information systems and integration of computer networks. Those elements were the beginning of a series of technology demand for new specialized processes in the offices: acquisition, installation, learning, maintenance and upgrading are referred by Sumner in [64]. In this phase the process for the issue of personal identification has begun to be performed electronically and automatized. During this process some phases also evolved; application phase did not suffer significant changes, documents to

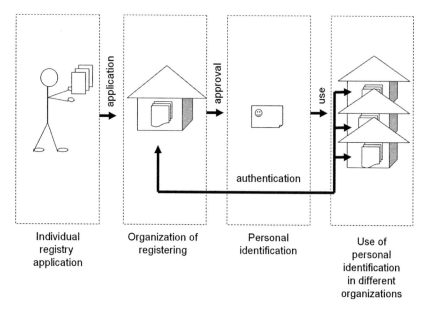

Figure 2.6: Second Age of the Process for the Issue of Personal Identity Documents

prove the name, date of birth and address were required. Registering phase have used information systems to store the user's personal information (except the photo) in a database; approval phase have used computer systems to print automatically the personal identity document in sealed paper which warranted the authenticity of the document. The use of electronic data interchange between organizations has been standardized since 1968 [41]. The standardization of data interchange performed information interchange via communication networks; the first specifications were for the file headers applicable to be switched (dial-up) and non switched (dedicated) communication networks as well as station-to-station and multi-station data communication systems. In its first edge, electronic data interchange between organizations was made through batch processes. The registering authority sent the information via the net after competition of the working day activities. Sometimes the batch process was applied weekly.

2.2.2 Process for the Issue of Personal Identity Documents on the Digital Age

The digital age is considered as the greatest computer revolution. The size of personal computers was reduced and they became a part of many people's life [68]. The computer networks became a very common structure to warrant the communication between entities. The increase of electronic information channels through internet forced to supplant most of paper-based in-

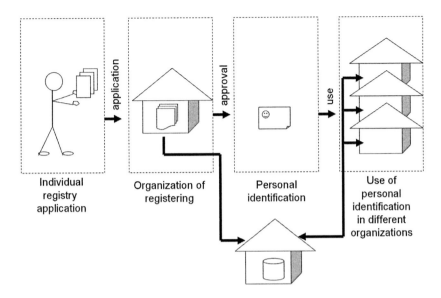

Figure 2.7: Personal Identity Process in the Third Phase

formation systems. The world wide web started its use for electronic information interchange between users and entities; the technology requirements such as people capacities increases the demand of automatizing the office processes and forcing the change from analog to digital technologies [65]. With the increase of computer networks use the security requirements for communication and data storage increased their complexity and technology needs. The use of secure nets was the first priority for most organizations. A process for the issue of personal identity documents evolved because of the new technology requirements and facilities. The first change in the personal identity document was the inclusion of some mechanisms to make them machine-readable and more secure; the use of bar codes was the beginning of series of security measures to warrant the authenticity of the identification document. A second mechanism is the magnetic stripe card, often called a magstripe, commonly used in credit cards, copy machine cards, transportation tickets or some other personal identity documents. The third mechanism used is the microchip in which the capacity of data store is larger than in the previously mentioned one.

2.3   Standardization of the Face Image

The International Civil Aviation Organization (ICAO) and the New Technologies Working Group (NTWG) accepted in the Berlin Resolution in June 2002 [48], that there are many advantages applied for face images, for example they are already socially, culturally accepted internationally and photographs do not disclose information that the person does not routinely disclose to the general public. The face image is non-intrusive and does not require new and costly enrollment procedures to be introduced. Many states maintain a legal database of face images captured as part of the digitized production of passport photographs which can be encoded into facial templates.

Since the introduction of that resolution, the face image is the mandatory biometric identifier to be included into digital identity documents. Different kinds of efforts have been made with the objective to ensure the quality of face images for digital data interchange, right printing and to provide facilities for face recognition.

In March 2003 the ICAO/NTWG recognizes in the New Orleans resolution "member states currently and will continue to utilize the face image as the primary identifier for MRTDs and as such endorses the use of standardized digitally stored face images as the globally interoperable biometric to support facial recognition technologies for machine assisted identity verification with MRTD; member states may use standardized digitally stored fingerprint and or iris images as additional globally interoperable biometrics in support of machine-assisted verification and/or identification; member states, in their initial deployment of MRTDs with biometrics identifiers, are encouraged to adopt contactless IC media of sufficient capacity to facilitate on-board storage of additional MRTD data and biometric identifiers." Different implementations have been applied to new passports. In Germany for example the new passport contains a contactless IC media and other security measures as is shown in Figure 2.5.

2.3.1 Logical Data Structure (LDS)

The Logical Data Structure (LDS) records identity details including biometric data. Its purpose is to facilitate confirmation of the presenter of an identification document or card as the rightful holder by machine-assisted means. The LDS data storage technologies are 2D barcodes, magnetic stripes, Integrated Circuit Chips (Contact IC or Contactless IC or both).

2.3.2 Guidelines for Taking Photographs to Maximize Face Recognition Results

A passport photograph must conform some requirements to be considered as being of good quality: it must be not older than 6 months, plain background light colored is required, photograph width must be 35-40mm, face takes up 70-80% of the photograph and it always must be visible. The individual has to look directly at the camera with a neutral expression with mouth closed, eyes open and clearly visible, no hair across the eyes, the head position frontal with no shadows or flash light on the face, the skin tones shall be natural, brightness and contrast must be appropriate, the photograph must be printed on high quality paper and at high resolution. Photographs taken with a digital camera must be high quality color and printed on photo quality paper, for wearers of glasses the eyes must be perfectly recognizable through the lenses with no flash reflection of the glasses, and tinted lenses with no heavy frames are not allowed. Except for religious reasons it is not permitted to use head covering [4].

2.3.3   Face Image Format for Interoperable Data Interchange

The face image format for Interoperable Data Interchange is defined in [4]. It specifies a record format for storing, recording, and transmitting the information from one or more face images, scene constraints, photographic properties and digital image attributes of the face images. This standard contains specifications related to the content attributes such as number of face images, number of feature points, gender, eye color, hair color, property mask (glasses, mustache, beard, teeth visible, blink, mouth open, left eye path, right eye path, dark glasses, feature distorting medical condition) and expression.

2.4   Potential Benefits of the Research Results

The metrics and applications developed with this thesis can become a basis for the further development of fast, automatized and objective quality determination of digital passport photographs and with this help to save time and money worldwide in the whole processes related to the facial image on the passport. Having initially an objective quality measurement when taking the photo, it is already possible to see if the image meets the high international demands and prevent lots of costs for issuing invalid document and getting problems when traveling. In addition the results can be used by the authorities, by airlines, etc.

2.5   Summary

In this Chapter the use of facial image in the different personal identification documents such as passport, visa, driver's license and personal identity card is described. An overview of passport's description and the history of the evolution of passports are given. As examples used are the United Kingdom's passport and the german electronic passport. Section 2.2 illustrates the influence of the computers to impulse the evolution of the processes for the issue of personal identity documents, the main changes of the processes from the first computer revolution to the digital age are described. In section 2.3 the efforts to standardize the face image as a biometric identificator in personal identification documents are depicted. This Chapter defines also the specifications of the face format for interoperable data interchange established in [4].

Table 2.1: UK Modern Passport Specifications

	First Modern Individual	Modern Family	Individual	Individual
Issued on	1915	Not registered	1981	1984
Country	United Kingdom	United Kingdom	United Kingdom	United Kingdom
Made officially by	British Nationality and Status Aliens Act 1914	League of Nations International Conference of Passports	Not specified	Ministers
Document's Characteristics	One page folded into 8 with a cardboard cover	Book-form, the now familiar blue with 32 pages	Not specified	Smooth transition to computerized passport
Holder Information Contained	Personal description, person's shape of face, features (nose: large, forehead: broad, eyes: small), complexion, color of eyes, distinguishing marks and height, occupation and country of residence	Personal information, family description	Not specified	Country of residence, occupation, distinguishing marks and height were omitted
Validity Period	Two years	Not specified	Not specified	Not specified
Renewed Period	Four two-year periods	Not specified	Not specified	Not specified
Additional Specifications	Holder's semi frontal photo in black and white	Family members frontal photo in black and white	Not specified	Not specified
Security Measure	Holder's signature	Not specified	Additional security measure to the laminate by incorporating a security laminate overprint	A new format blue passport

Table 2.2: UK Second Generation of Modern Passport Specifications

	Second Generation Modern Individual Passport	Frequent Travelers
Year	1972	1973
Country	United Kingdom	United Kingdom
Made official by	Not specified	Not specified
Document Characteristics	Book-form 30 pages	Book-form 94 pages
Holder Information Contained	Not specified	Not specified
Validity Period	10 years for persons aged 16 or over	Not specified
Renewed Period	Not specified	Not specified
Additional Specifications	Holder's semi frontal photo in black and white, a woman's maiden name was no longer shown on page 1 and the color of eyes on page 2 was no longer included	Not specified
Security Measure	Blue security paper incorporating a special water-mark	Starting in 1975, photographs in passports were laminated to prevent exchanging the original photograph against one of a pretended holder

Table 2.3: Individual Machine Readable Passport

Individual Machine Readable Passport	
Year	1988
Country	United Kingdom
Made official by	Glasgow Passport Office, International Civil Aviation Organisation (ICAO), Council of Ministers of the European Community
Document Characteristics	1988 New style, burgundy red, machine-readable United Kingdom Passport. Certain information inside the passport were translated into the official languages of the European Community. The UK passport with the EU references was first issued in December 1997. Two types of machine-readable passports are produced: the European Community/ Union Format Passport and the Non EC/EU 'looka-like' passport
Holder Information Contained	Not specified
Validity Period	Not specified
Renewed Period	Not specified
Additional Specifications	Not specified
Security Measure	The machine-readable passports have as a key feature the machine-readable strip at the bottom of the details page (inside the back cover). This means that the passport details can be read by a machine at passport control enabling immediate cross-referencing with immigration computers.

Table 2.4: UK's Vision in 1998 of Passports for the Future

Passports for the Future	
Year	1998
Country	United Kingdom
Made official by	International Civil Aviation Organization (ICAO), Council of Members of the European Community
Document Characteristics	Not specified
Holder Information Contained	Not specified
Validity Period	Not specified
Renewed Period	Not specified
Additional Specifications	Not specified
Security Measure	The transfer of the holder's personal data from the inside of the back cover to the last page in the passport. A digitally printed face image of the holder (instead of a glued-in photograph) is used. The holder's signature is digitally captured onto the passport. The personal identification page is protected by a clear laminate which incorporates a transparent optically variable device which protects the portrait. The identification page is further protected by a series of laser perforations. Both inner surfaces of the front and back cover use intaglio printing. The resultant ridged profile is detectable by checking the fingertips. These features and others have been designed to prevent photo substitution, page splitting, and other attempts of counterfeiting, and forgery. The 'data page' is now on page 31 and all information including the holder's signature is covered by a security laminate

Table 2.5: Security Features of the German Electronic Passport of 2005

	Security Feature	Description
1	Holographic portrait	Is a second, holographic image of the passport or identity-card holder's photograph becomes visible to the right of the conventional picture when the passport data page or the ID card is viewed from a shallow angle
2	3D German eagle	A three-dimensional image of the German eagle in red can be detected from a specific viewing angle
3	Kinematic structures	Kinematic structures are arranged above the conventional photograph; their central element is a German eagle surrounded by twelve stars
4	Macrolettering and microlettering	There are kinematic structures on the left edge of the conventional photograph consisting of a curved band of macrolettering with the text "BUNDESREPUBLIK DEUTSCHLAND" (Federal Republic of Germany)
5	Holographic representation of the machine-readable lines	The two machine-readable lines of the data page or ID card are repeated as holograms, these are situated above the conventional machine-readable lines
6	Machine verifiable structure	This structure does no contain any personal or document-related data
7	Surface embossing	The data page or ID card is embedded into a special laminate
8	Security printing with multi color guilloches	Guilloches are protective patterns made up fine, interlacing curved lines in which different colored structures fit together perfectly to form a balanced overall picture
9	Laser lettering	The passport holder's family name are laser engraved into the identification document material at the right hand edge of the photograph
10	Watermark	when light shines through the paper of the data page or ID card, a multitonal watermark can be detected in the form of stylized eagles distributed over the surface

Chapter 3

Theoretical Framework

In this chapter the frequent and important terms Quality, Biometrics and Image Quality are discussed, different types of quality measurement are described. Major information is given, that is necessary to interpret the results from following chapters with the adequate approach. The implementation of selected algorithms and formulas for image quality determination introduced in this Chapter are explained in Chapter 6

3.1 Quality

This thesis is fundamentally based on a certain understanding of *"Quality"*, thus this chapter deals with this term. After giving an introduction of the concept, a new definition is proposed.

3.1.1 Quality Control History

During the early days of manufacturing, an operative's work was inspected and a decision made whether to accept or reject it. Due to the fast growing manufacturing capacities the inspection also got a bigger and bigger importance, so that full time inspection jobs were created [51]. In the 1920's statistical theory began to be applied effectively to quality control, and in 1924 Shewhart made the first sketch of a modern control chart. His work was later developed by Deming and the early work of Shewhart, Deming, Dodge and Romig constitutes much of what today comprises the theory of statistical process control (SPC). However, there was little use of these techniques in manufacturing companies until the late 1940's [51].

The Japanese manufacturing industry was the pioneer in implementing a standardized manufacturing system [24]. It was developed by the Department of Defense of the USA. The system was called "Quality Assurance". In the 1980s and early 1990s the quality concept gained more attention from the industry in USA. Quality revolution begun when it was one of the central business research topics. The most famous author, known as the father of "Quality Revolution", was Philip Crosby. His legacy to quality is the concept of zero defects.

3.1.2   The Term "Quality"

According to [9] quality is an inherent or distinguishing characteristic; Crosby specifies that quality is the conformance of requirements [12]. It means when requirements are not met then it is a nonconforming product and consequently does not posses any quality; Crosby's quality conception is binary. One of the problems working with quality is to determine the acceptance grade of conformance. For Crosby there is no tolerance to any defect, Crosby's quality is total, there is no partial quality for him. Crosby in his different publications defends his theory of quality culture change. He emphasizes the use of the "Absolutes of Quality Management" [13]. To obtain products with total quality, the absolutes are:

1. *Quality is conformance to requirements, not as 'goodness' or 'elegance'.* If we want our people to do "it" right the first time, they have to understand clearly what "it" is.

2. *The system of quality is prevention, not appraisal.* We have to vaccinate the company against problems, not to spend our time finding and fixing errors.

3. *The performance standard must be Zero Defects, not "that's close enough".* Quality is defect-free, not acceptable quality levels. If an error is planned to occur, then it will occur as planned.

4. *The measurement of quality is the price of non-conformance, not indices.* All the costs of not doing things right must be tabulated, so management gets to know where to take action.

When referring to quality, there is one international standard dealing with quality, that is most known: ISO 9000. This standard, in its definition, determines the degrees of quality by the series of characteristics in which it must comply with the required specifications [24]. This definition completely opposes the radical concept of Crosby. The measurement of quality can be composed by the union of different degrees of compliance of quality. The degree of acceptance of quality must be determined by the quality managers depending on its degree of application. This means that quality can be customized.

3.1.3   Quality Measurement

Concerning the measurement of quality this thesis refers to the definition in [6]: Quality can be measured and it should be calculated according to the requirement's specifications of the standards related. In chapter four the *Achto Cualli* method is explained in detail. It contains a series of precepts that gives a guide to find the requirement's specifications that are measurable.

3.1.4   Subjective Measurement of Quality

Subjective measurement estimates a variable value for quality of an image through different studies such as direct estimation, visual analog scale or adjectival scales [66]. There are graded descriptions of acceptance or rejection to assign the values. For each scale the human opinion plays the main role. Subjective measures are useful for quantifying attributes of image usage that cannot be directly measured through objective means. The Mean Opinion Score (MOS) uses subjective tests (opinionated scores) that are mathematically averaged to obtain a quantitative indicator of the image quality [66]. MOS objective is to determine what level of statistical acceptance can be achieved while maintaining adequate subjective image quality. MOS method has been used mainly in customer service quality measurements and in marketing processes.

3.1.5   Subjective Quality Scales

The methods commonly used to measure subjective quality of speech and video images have been standardized and recommended by the International Telecommunications Union (ITU) [66]. Its works include series of recommended scales, based on results of laboratory experiments to test the quality of monitor's resolution and contrast. These experiments were conducted using some methods designed for the European Broadcasting Union (EBU). Some other methods were designed for the ITU. The first scale is the five-grade image impairment [66]. It represents the degree of visibility annoyance caused by one or more impairments with respect to a reference picture scale. In Table 3.1 the scored values can be found.

Table 3.1: Five-Grade Image Impairment Scale

Score	Description
5	imperceptible
4	perceptible, but not annoying
3	slightly annoying
2	annoying
1	very annoying

The double stimulus continuous quality-scale (DSCQS) method is cyclic in that the observer is asked to view a pair of pictures [66], each from the same source but one via process under examination and another directly from the source. He is asked to assess the quality of both. Figure 3.1 shows the rating scale. In an adjectival categorical judgment scale [66], the observer assigns an image or image sequence to one of a set of categories which typically is defined in semantic terms that reflect judgments of an attribute. Categorical scales assess image quality and impairment. Table 3.2 yields a distribution of judgments across scale categories for each condition; these categories may report the existence and direction of perceptible differences (e.g. less, same, more) or judgments of extent and direction.

Subjective measurements correspond to the observer's overall perception of an image. This perception is the broadest scope of image quality as it includes any factor of influencing the observer's perception of a picture. Subjective metrics carry the risk of wrong interpretations of perception scores. It must be specified how good a good image is or how bad a bad image is. It means that an equilibrated quality metric should be compounded for a combination of the two

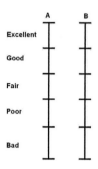

Figure 3.1: Double Stimulus Quality Scale

Table 3.2: Five-Grade Image Quality Scale

Score	Description
5	Excellent
4	Good
3	Fair
2	Poor
1	Bad

Table 3.3: Quality Comparison Scale

Score	Description
-3	Much worse
-2	Worse
-1	Slightly worse
0	The same
+1	Slightly better
+2	Better
+3	Much better

types of metrics: objective and subjective. It may not be possible to fully characterize image quality by just one type of measurement: both types of measurements are not contradictory but complement each other.

3.2   Biometrics

Biometrics is a general term used alternatively to describe an attribute or a process. As characteristic, a biometric is a measurable biological (anatomical and physiological) and behavioral characteristic that can be used for automated recognition. As a process, a biometric is an automated method for recognizing an individual based on measurable biological (anatomical and physiological) and behavioral characteristics. [59]

For the European Parliament Committee on Citizen's Freedoms and Rights, Justice and Home Affairs a biometric is *a physical or biological feature or attribute that can be measured. It can be used as a means of proving that you are who you claim to be, or as means of proving that you are who you claim to be, or as a means of proving without revealing your identity that you have a certain right (e.g. access) just like a PIN (personal identification number) or password* [22].
The terms biometrics and biometric identification are commonly used referring to the identification of an individual. There are different terms related to the identification of an individual that have to be distinguished:

- Biometrics

- Biometric data

- Biometric characteristic

- Biometric feature

- Biometric indicator

- Biometric measure

- Biometric identification

Biometric feature, biometric indicator or biometric characteristic are different designations, given to refer to the physical or biological features that characterize an individual. They are any human physical or biological feature that can be measured and used for the purpose of automated or semi-automated identification. Such features can be categorized as physiological (e.g. height, weight, face, iris or retina.) or behavioral (e.g. voice, signature or keystroke sequence). Some biometric features are persistent over time while others change. All biometric features are deemed 'unique' but some are less 'distinct' than others and thus less useful for automated identification purposes [22]. The distinctiveness of any biometric feature depends also on the effectiveness of the sampling technique used to measure it as well as on the efficiency of the matching process used to declare a 'match' between two samples. Biometric data is the quantitative or qualitative information correspondent to the biometric identificator. Biometric technologies are supposed to bring a reduction in error and fraud to the processes of identification and authentication through stronger confidence in the authenticity of official documents like passports and driving licenses [22].

Biometric identification works in four stages: enrollment, storage, acquisition and matching. Features extracted during enrollment and acquisition stages are often transformed (through a non-reversible process) into templates in an effort to facilitate the storage and matching processes. Templates contain less data than the original sample, they are usually manufacturer-dependent and therefore not generally interoperable with those of other manufacturers. Templates or full samples thus acquired may then be held in storage that is either centralized (e.g. in a database) or decentralized (e.g. on a smart card). As a consequence of the statistical nature of the acquisition and matching stages, biometric systems are never 100% accurate. There are two kinds of possible errors: a false match, and a false non-match. These errors vary from one biometric technology to another and depend on the threshold used to determine a 'match'. This threshold is set by the operators depending on the application.

There are seven widely-accepted criteria to assess biometric technologies: universality, distinctiveness, permanence, collectability, performance, acceptability and resistance to circumvention. The degree, to which each biometric technology fulfills a given criterion, varies. However it is only useful to compare the technologies based on the criteria once a specific application and a concrete identification purpose have been set. For example a convenience application (e.g. controlling access to food in the student cafeteria) may tolerate a significant error rate while a high-security application (such as controlling access to a nuclear site) would require minimal error rates. There are currently few biometric applications that have millions of enrolled individuals and thousands of deployed devices. Those, that do exist are typically in law enforcement and in certain civil areas. Physical access control (access to a site) is another area that has been developed and logical access (in particular on-line identity) is forecast to be a fast-growing use of biometrics in the future. More importantly, the integration of biometrics into passports and visas will be the first truly large-scale deployment in the European Union. It still remains to be seen whether biometric applications will be deployed where individuals voluntarily participate because they find the application beneficial and convenient [22].

3.2.1   Classification of Biometric Technologies

Biometric technologies are automated methods of verifying or recognizing the identity of a living person based on a physiological or behavioral characteristic [20]. Since a person's biometric features are a part of his or her body, they will always be with that person wherever he/she goes and enable to prove his or her identity. Biometric technologies may be used in three ways:

- to verify that people are who they claim to be

- to discover the identity of unknown people

- to screen people against a watch-list

The biometric technologies are classified according to the different physiological and behavioral characteristics currently used [20]:

- Face

- Fingerprint

- Voice

- Iris

- Retina

- Hand

- Handwriting

- Keystroke

- Finger shape

- Gait

- Ear shape

- Head resonance

- Optical skin reflectance

- Body odor

For Wayman et al [20] a sub-classification of the biometric technologies can be organized by the type of measurement of the biometric indicator, for example a single one-dimensional signal (voice); several simultaneous one-dimensional signals (hand writing); a single two-dimensional image (fingerprint); multiple two dimensional measures (hand geometry); a time series of two-dimensional images (face and iris); or a three-dimensional image (some facial recognition systems).

3.2.2 Face Image as Biometric Identifier

The identification of individuals can be achieved more securely by using a combination of two kinds of factors: an external object they possess and physiological characteristic they have. The use of biometrics in personal identity documents binds the individual identity to the document. Biometrics are the implementation of different algorithms of recognizing and authenticating the identity of a living person through the measurement of unique physiological or behavioral characteristics such as face, finger print, iris, voice, signature, etc. [48] [71] [33] [17].

Modern personal identity documents can include some potential characteristics stored on a chip. This information includes e.g. holder's digital photo, personal information and biometric identifiers, digital certificate of authentication and an electronic signature. All identity documents have some holder's information in common such as first and last name, date of birth etc. but the most important mandatory identifier always required through the history of the personal identity documents is the face image [17] [71] [22]. Writing about personal identity implies referencing a merely unavoidable to avoid fact. After 11th September 2001, biometrics became highly impulse in their implementation to identify and verify the personal identity of an individual in international borders worldwide.

In June 2004 the European Union Home Affairs Council determined in the 2588th Council meeting [21] that the EU citizens' passports should contain as first mandatory biometric identifier a face identifier and an optional one mostly fingerprints. After that meeting the design of quality of face images and finger prints to ensure personal identity documents such as passports have been started, produced and controlled. The international interest in standarizing the biometric identifiers gained more support and many international work groups were integrated to define the conformance requirements to accomplish, meet or exceed the international standards specifications.

3.3   Image Quality

According to Keelan [37] "the quality of an image is defined to be an impression of its merit or excellence, as perceived by an observer neither associated with the act of photography, nor closely involved with the subject matter depicted". For Janssen [35] image quality can be "the adequacy of this image as input to visual perception" or "the adequacy of an image as input to visual perception is given by the discriminability and identifiability of the items depicted in the image". In Ikram's opinion [1] image quality can be defined as "an indicator of the relevance of the information presented by an image to the task we seek to accomplish using this image". It can be considered that image quality is determined by the degree a set of inherent characteristics of an image fulfills the requirements established. In this thesis the requirements seeking to be accomplished are analyzed and detailed in the next Chapter.

3.3.1   Measurement of Image Quality

Keelan states, that to determine the quality of an image, there are many factors or attributes that can be considered [37]. There are many attributes contributing to perceive image quality. Their classification is made according to the nature of the attribute; they can be artifactual, preferential, aesthetic and personal. Artifactual attributes are degrading quality when they are detectable, preferential attributes are always evident and possess an optimum position, aesthetic attributes are related to the artistic merit. A better result of the quality measurement is the determination of relations between scale values of the attributes and objective measures. Methods to measure the image quality can be divided into two categories: objective and subjective [44]. An objective measurement estimates a constant value for quality of an image through different mathematical algorithms. A subjective measurement estimates a variable value for quality of an image through different studies such as direct estimation, visual analog scale or adjectival scales in which the human opinion of the image plays the main role.

3.3.2   Objective Measurement

The objective measurement can be classified if a reference image without distortion is available to be compared with a distorted image. Objective measurement arises from the combination of their objective nature and their correlation with attributes of image quality. Most of the objective metrics are determined by direct experimental methods. An objective metric has a single number determined through objective means from attributes of quality within an image, accounting for its viewing conditions and the properties of the human visual system [76]. The following functions represent the measures used to determine the errors or distortion factors of an image.

3.3.2.1   Error Functions

Generally the error function gives a measure of the overall error when a number n is used to represent an entire distribution. The error function minimum is obtained and that value is the corresponding measure of spread; some error functions occur throughout statistics and some others occur through special properties.

3.3.2.2   Mean Squared Error (MSE)

The Mean Squared Error (MSE) is a statistical measure. It compares on a pixel-by-pixel basis the luminance patterns from the original signal with a distorted version. It is calculated as shown in formula (3.1) from [35].

$$MSE(I, I') = \frac{1}{NM} \sum_{i=1}^{N} \sum_{j=1}^{M} [I'(i,j) - I(i,j)]^2 \tag{3.1}$$

where $I(i,j)$ represents the original image luminance and $I'(i,j)$ represents the distorted image luminance for the pixel located at row i and column j and N and M represent the number of rows and columns of the images. MSE is a measure to calculate the image quality difference between two similar images but it cannot be used to predict which of the two versions of the image is better.

3.3.2.3   Root Mean Squared Error (RMSE)

The Root Mean Squared Error (RMSE) is one of the most common measures of success for numeric prediction. This value is computed by taking the average of the squared differences between each computed value (c_i) and its corresponding correct value (a_i) where i varies from 1 to n. The same dimensionality as the actual and predicted values as shown in (3.2) is represented in a simplified metric from [37]. This formula is based on the root mean square deviation (RMSD).

$$RMSE = \sqrt[2]{\frac{(a_1 - c_1)^2 + (a_2 - c_2)^2 + ... + (a_n - c_n)^2}{n}} \tag{3.2}$$

3.3.2.4   Mean Absolute Error (MAE)

The Mean Absolute Error (MAE) is another interpretation of mean deviation. It is a measure of dispersion derived from the average deviation of observations from some central value, such deviations being taken as absolute. The mean absolute error function is: (3.3)

$$MAE_i = \frac{1}{n} \sum_{j=1}^{n} | P_{(ij)} - T_j |$$ (3.3)

where $P_{(ij)}$ is the value predicted by the central value i for sample case j (out of n sample cases); and T_j is the target value for sample case j. For a perfect fit, $P_{(ij)} = T$ and $MAE_i = 0$. The MAE_i index ranges from zero to infinity; a zero MAE represents a perfect fit.

3.3.2.5   Noise Functions

Fisher in [23] defines noise as a general term for the deviation of a signal away from its "true" value. In the case of images this leads to pixel values (or other measurements) that are different from their expected values. The causes of noise can be random factors such as thermal noise in the sensor, or minor scene events such as dust or smoke. Noise can also represent systematic but unmodeled events such as short therm lighting variations or quantization. Noise might be reduced or removed using a noise reduction method. Noise can become a significant problem in digital imaging systems [50]. Images are often degraded by some random errors; they can occur during image capturing, transmission, or processing. Noise is usually described by its probabilistic characteristics [44].

3.3.2.6   Signal to Noise Ratio (SNR)

Signal to Noise Ratio (SNR) is a measure of the relative strength of the interesting and uninteresting (noise) part of a signal. In signal processing SNR is usually expressed in decibels as the ratio of the power of signal and noise is expressed as can be seen in Formula (3.4) from [23]. With statistical noise the SNR can be defined as 10 times the common logarithm of the ratio of the standard deviations of the Power P from signal and noise.

$$SNR = 10log_{10} \frac{P_{signal}}{P_{noise}}$$ (3.4)

3.3.2.7   Peak Signal to Noise Ratio (PSNR)

The Peak Signal to Noise Ratio (PSNR) is a statistical measure. Non-human vision system picture differencing measurement derived from the ratio of the peak signal to the root mean [57]. It is considered as a normalization of MSE [35] and is presented in decibels and calculated by dividing the square of the luminance range R of the display device by the MSE as shown in (3.5).

$$PSNR = 10\log_{10}\frac{R^2}{MSE} \tag{3.5}$$

This formula is used to measure the quality of reconstruction in image compression, its typical values are between 30 and 40 db.

3.3.3 Metrics for Image Attributes

A passport photo has some attributes that have a high influence in its perception. The main focus lies on algorithms allowing a quality assessment using the existing resources; the assessment of the following aspects of quality metrics is examined:

- Contrast

- Lightness - Brightness

- Noise

- Blur

- Color Space

3.3.4 Contrast

The contrast measurement has been conducted according to three different approaches [29], [52], [10]:

1. Human Visual System (*HVS*)

2. Physical

3. First Order Statistics

3.3.4.1 Human Visual System

The approaches described are based on the modeling of the human visual perception system (HVS). All definitions proceed in the local frequency space, so the Fourier Transformation methods are implemented. For both methods it holds that $f(x, y)$ represents the picture in the local area, while $F(k_x, k_y) = F(k_r, k_\varphi)$ represents the Fourier transformation in a spatial frequency area. k_x, k_y both represent the spatial frequencies in a cartesian plane, while k_r, k_φ represent the spatial frequency in even polar coordinates.

3.3.4.2 Band-Limited Contrast

According to [55] the contrast of a complex representation in the local frequency. Space can be defined as:

$$C(k_x, k_y) = 2 \left| \frac{F(k_x, k_y)}{F(k_x = 0, k_y = 0)} \right|^2 \tag{3.6}$$

A contrast number for a picture can be defined by the sum of all frequency values, w is the width and h is the height of the picture [55]:

$$K_{\text{Hess}} = \frac{\sum_{k_x} \sum_{k_y} C(k_x, k_y)}{w * h} \tag{3.7}$$

3.3.4.3 Local Band-Limited Contrast

To allow the definiton of the local band-limited contrast for a complex representation, a band-limited version of the picture $A(k_r, k_\varphi)$ in the local frequency space is calculated first. This can be achieved by applying in the local frequency space a radial-symmetric filter $G(k_r)$ to the Fourier transformed value $F(k_r, k_\varphi)$ of the picture. It has been proved to be advisable to consider bandwidth of about an octave, each since they contain about the same energy values. For a detailed description of the biological reasons for this selection see [52] and the references mentioned there. So the band-limited picture in the local frequency space can be represented by:

$$A(k_x, k_y) \equiv A(k_r, k_\varphi) = F(k_r, k_\varphi)\, G(k_r), \text{with:} k_r = \sqrt{k_x^2 + k_y^2} \tag{3.8}$$

$$k_\varphi = \arctan \frac{k_y}{k_x} \tag{3.9}$$

$$F(k_r, k_\varphi) = \mathcal{F}\{f(x, y)\} \tag{3.10}$$

The Fourier transformed value of the picture results in:

$$F(k_r, k_\varphi) = L_i(k_r, k_\varphi) + \sum_{j=i}^{n-1} A_j(k_r, k_\varphi) + H_n(k_r, k_\varphi) \tag{3.11}$$

where $L_i(k_r, k_\varphi)$ represents the low-pass rate, $H_n(k_r, k_\varphi)$ the high-pass rate, and $\sum_{j=i}^{n-1} A_j(k_r, k_\varphi)$ the band-pass rate of the Fourier transformed value. The high-pass rate generally contains a low energy or information content and will be disregarded in the following. The low-pass rate is essential for further consideration (high information content) and will be retained. The band-pass rates A_j are determined using a cos-log filter of a bandwidth of one octave, each centered around the 2^j-th local frequency:

$$G_j(k_r) = 0.5[1 + \cos\{\pi(\log_2 r + j)\}] \tag{3.12}$$

This allows to define a local band-limited contrast for the local space:

$$c_i(x,y) \;=\; \frac{a_i(x,y)}{l_i(x,y)} = \frac{a_i(x,y)}{l_0(x,y) + \sum\limits_{j=1}^{i-1} a_j(x,y)} \tag{3.13}$$

$$=\; \frac{l_{i+1}(x,y) - l_i(x,y)}{l_i(x,y)} = \frac{l_{i+1}(x,y)}{l_i(x,y)} - 1 \tag{3.14}$$

The second formula shows the advantage that just one low-level filter must be implemented. Finally it has to be considered, if a contrast definition geared to the human visual perception system is actually suited for the evaluation of face recognition algorithms (Principal Component Analyzing (PCA), eigenfaces methods, etc.). It is *a priori* not evident that the contrast perception by the human eye and brain is similar to the contrast perception by a face recognition algorithm based on PCA, eigenfaces or other methods. Therefore there is no real legitimacy to use such a contrast definition [27].

3.3.4.4 Physical Approach

Two definitions have been commonly used for measuring the contrast of test targets. The contrast C of a periodic pattern such as sinusoidal grating is measured with:

- Contrast according to Michelson [52]

- Contrast according to Weber [52]

Michelson defines the contrast through:

$$C_M = \frac{I_{max} - I_{min}}{I_{max} + I_{min}}; \quad \text{with:} C_M \in [0,1] \tag{3.15}$$

where I_{max} and I_{min} are the maximum and minimum intensity value.

Weber defines contrast through:

$$C_W = \frac{I - \overline{I}}{\overline{I}}; \quad \text{with: } C_W \in [0, +\infty) \tag{3.16}$$

where I is the local intensity value and $\overline{I}$ is the mean value of the intensity distribution. However it must be considered, that the two formulae characterize the intensity variations around a mean value but they are not equivalent. This can be seen because the parameters do not coincide. The parameters of the Michelson formula ranges from $[0,1]$ while the range in Weber's formula are from $[-1, +\infty)$. A Michelson contrast of 0 means that there is no contrast independent of the intensity whereas a contrast of 1 means that there is a maximal difference between the maximal and the minimal intensity [52]. Provided that black is encoded with 0 the Michelson formula says that every point unequal to black shows a maximum contrast in a completely black environment independent of its intensity. A Weber contrast of -1 means that a black point is in a non-black environment. A Weber contrast of 0 means that there is no

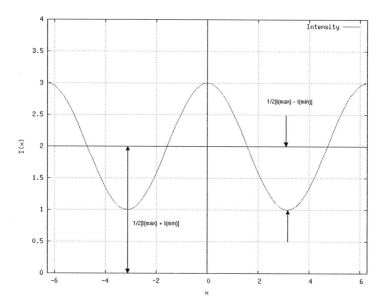

Figure 3.2: Definition of Michelson Contrast

Table 3.4: Limit Values of Michelson Contrast

Value	Meaning
0	No Contrast. Same background and foreground
1	Maximum Contrast. No black foreground in black background

contrast, i.e. that the local point shows the same intensity as the background, and an infinite contrast means that a clear point is on a black background in which the brightness and the intensity of the local point are irrelevant.

A contrast of a picture can be determined by defining an operator window of the value $(2n + 1)*(2n+1)$. Tests have shown that values of $3*3$ and $5*5$ respectively deliver optimal results. This window is shifted over the picture, line by line, top down, and thereby one of the two formulas is used pixel by pixel. In other words, the operator window cuts a $(2n+1)*(2n+1)$ big picture detail to which one of the Formula 3.15 or 3.5 is applied. The result of the operation is allocated to the middle window pixel

P($(2n + 1)/2 + 1$,$(2n + 1)/2 + 1$), the operation result is assigned. In this way an output

Table 3.5: Limit Values of Weber Contrast

Value	Meaning
-1	Black point in no black background
0	No contrast. Same background and foreground
$+\infty$	No black point in black background

picture is generated from the original picture which gives locally some information about the contrast; see Figure 3.3. The easiest way to allocate a global contrast value to the picture is

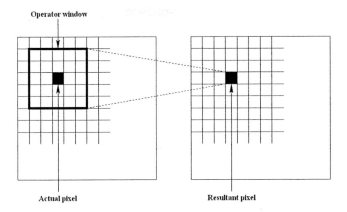

Figure 3.3: Local Contrast Operator Organizes the Actual Resultant Pixel in a Contrast Bitmap

to calculate the arithmetic average of the output, respectively contrast picture:

$$K_{\text{Image}} = \frac{\sum_{i=1}^{w*h} K_i}{w * h} \tag{3.17}$$

where w is the picture width, h the picture height, and K_i the contrast value of the i-th pixel of the picture, calculated following Michelson or Weber. The result is scaled to the picture size allowing a comparison between pictures of different size.

3.3.5   Brightness

Brightness is the measurement of the gray level intensity associated with an individual pixel or region of the image [10]. The presented approach based on first-order statistics has been developed by the U.S. finance department for the purpose of assessing the quality of scanned checks. For a detailed discussion of the presented methods see [10, 61].

3.3.6   Brightness Type I

In this metric, the pixel values will be added and normalized onto the pixel values and the maximum

$$\overline{H} = \frac{\sum\limits_{i=1}^{w*h} P(i)}{w * h * I_{max}}, \text{ with:}$$

$$P(i) : \text{Grey value} \tag{3.18}$$

$$I_{max} : \text{Max. intensity value}$$

$$w : \text{Image width}$$

$$h : \text{Image height}$$

The metric value varies between 0 and 1, whereas 0 means the absolute darkness and 1 is the maximum brightness.

3.3.7   Brightness Type II

The method is applied to gray value pictures. In a first step the gray value histogram of the picture is determined. From this histogram all brightness or gray values are gained. The assumption is again that black is coded with 0 and white with I_{max}. With the definition for medium white:

$$\overline{W} = \frac{\sum\limits_{i=\epsilon*I_{max}}^{I_{max}} i * G(i)}{w * h}, \text{ with:}$$

$$0 \leq \epsilon \leq 1 \tag{3.19}$$

$$I_{max} : \text{max. Intensity value}$$

$$G(i) : \text{Gray value histogram}$$

$$w : \text{Image width}$$

$$h : \text{Image height}$$

and the definition of the average brightness (lightness)

$$\overline{H} = \frac{\overline{W}}{I_{max}} \tag{3.20}$$

The average contrast of the picture is defined by:

$$\overline{C} = \frac{\overline{W} - \overline{S}}{I_{max}} \tag{3.21}$$

Within the method presented in this section the picture is regarded as too light if:

$$1)\overline{H} > \Theta_{\overline{H},max} \tag{3.22}$$

$$2)\overline{C} < \Theta_{\overline{C},min} \tag{3.23}$$

That is when the middle brightness lies above the brightness threshold *and* at the same time the contrast value lies below the contrast threshold. The picture is regarded as too dark if:

$$\overline{H} > \Theta_{\overline{H},min} \tag{3.24}$$

i.e. independently of the contrast value the picture is always too dark if the average brightness value lies below the brightness threshold.

3.3.8 Impulsive Noise (Salt-Pepper Noise)

Noise is a general term for the deviation of a signal away from its "true" value. In the case of images, this leads to pixel values (or other measurements) that are different from their expected values. The causes of noise can be random factors such as thermal noise in the sensor or minor scene events, such as dust or smoke. Noise can also represent systematic, but unmodeled events such as short term lighting variations or quantization. Noise might be reduced or removed using a noise reduction method. This section describes approaches dealing with the determination of noise metrics ('salt and pepper' and impulse noise respectively) as well as blur metrics. The focus lies on a survey of the facts, efficient in calculation and not on developing models describing noise phenomena. The impulsive noise metric presented here was created by Juan Guerrero [27] and is based on an adaptive median filter that uses a switching scheme based on local statistics characters proposed by Wang Li-Qiang et al in [40]. In order to decide if a certain pixel of the picture contains noise or not its immediate environment is examined. This immediate environment is defined by the size of a window in which the pixel in question is the central window pixel. So a $(2n + 1) * (2n + 1)$ big window is examined surrounding the original and the actual pixel of the noise-added picture:

$$W = \{(u,v)|-n \le u \le n, -n \le v \le n\} \tag{3.25}$$

To decide if the central pixel has noise or not, the pixels contained in the window undergo a median operation:

$$M(x,y) = median(\{P(x-u,y-v)|(u,v) \in W\}) \tag{3.26}$$

where (x,y) represent picture coordinates and (u,v) window coordinates. For the pixel in question $P(x-u,y-v)$ the difference between its value and the result of the median operation is defined as:

$$d(x,y) = |M(x,y) - P(x,y)| \tag{3.27}$$

To be able to decide whether there is added noise to the pixel a threshold is assumed:

$$\Theta(x,y) = \overline{P}(x,y) + k\,\sigma(x,y) \tag{3.28}$$

in which k is a free parameter to be determined, $\overline{P}(x, y)$ the mean value of all pixels contained in the window

$$\overline{P}(x, y) = \frac{\sum\limits_{u,v} \{P(x - u, y - v)|(u, v) \in W\}}{(2n + 1)^2} \qquad (3.29)$$

and $\sigma(x, y)$ the standard deviation of the window pixels

$$\sigma(x, y) = \sqrt{\frac{\sum\limits_{u,v \in W} (P(x - u, y - v) - \overline{P}(x, y))^2}{(2n + 1)^2 - 1}} \qquad (3.30)$$

The following criteria determines, if the current pixel has noise or if it is regarded:

$$\widehat{P}(x, y) = \begin{cases} M(x, y) & \text{if } d(x, y) \geq \Theta(x, y) \\ P(x, y) & \text{if } d(x, y) < \Theta(x, y) \end{cases} \qquad (3.31)$$

$\widehat{P}(x, y)$ represents the noise-free new pixel. For values of $k = 0.5$, 1, 1.5, 2 and n = 1, 2 and 3 tests were carried out with the picture material of the FERET database. The best results were obtained for values of k = 1 and n = 2.

In accordance with formula 3.32 from [27] the sum from all pixels over the rushed pixels released give as result the total number of image pixels to be normalized.

$$R_{\text{noise}} = \frac{\sum\limits_{x,y} \delta_{\widehat{P}(x,y),M(x,y)}}{w * h} \qquad (3.32)$$

in which $\delta_{i,j}$ is the Delta value and is correlated through the discrete version of Delta called Kronecker-Delta and is defined as:

$$\delta_{\widehat{P}(x,y),M(x,y)} = \begin{cases} 1 & \text{if } \widehat{P}(x, y) = M(x, y) \\ 0 & \text{if } \widehat{P}(x, y) \neq M(x, y) \end{cases} \qquad (3.33)$$

3.3.9   Blur Measurement

A picture is fuzzy if the high-frequency part of the local frequency spectrum is damped or cleared. There are different reasons for fuzzy figures like, e.g., fuzziness by motion due to relative movements between camera and object, or out-of-focus fuzziness due to wrongly tuned camera and/or lenses errors, or resulting from the digital image processing like picture compression. In this section a method for assessing the fuzziness without needing a reference photo is introduced. Furthermore, no knowledge of the image content or the type of fuzziness is necessary. The objective of this metric is to proof the blur existence in an image. Blur metrics are defined in the local space, so that no Fourier transformation is necessary, reducing the calculating time considerably. The fuzziness of a picture is mainly striking along the edges of objects or textured regions. The method is based on verifying a smoothing of the edges caused by the fuzziness. The algorithm consists of the following steps:

1. By means of a an edge detector (e.g. vertical Soebel filter) the vertical edges are determined.

2. In each row being part of the vertical edge and beginning from the vertical position, which the edging detector supplied, the extents edge certainly increases.

3. The width of the edge is defined as the distance between the direct local maximum and minimum and the edge position represents a local fuzziness rate.

4. The global fuzziness rate is formed as an arithmetic mean value comprising all local fuzziness rates.

Figures 3.4 and 3.5 show the algorithm and an example as presented in [43] where TotBM means Total of blur measurement, NbEdges means No. of edges. The author suggests that the detection of vertical edges is sufficient for defining a good blur metrics using a no-reference perceptual blur metric. In any case this statement should be controlled concerning facial images since most of the edges and lines in the face are horizontal and not vertical. So it could be possible that the algorithm must be modified to use horizontal or both edge types for calculating the metrics value.

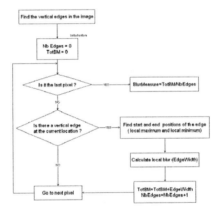

Figure 3.4: Blur Metrics Algorithm

In the example of Figure 3.5 for the edge location $P1$, the local maximum $P2$ defines the start position while the local minimum $P2'$ defines the end position. The edge width is $P2' - P2$ or in this case 11 pixels. For color images blur is measured on the luminance component Y. The blur metric proposed for [43] can be interpreted as follows:

$$BlurMeasure = TotBM/NbEdges \quad and \quad TotBM = \sum_{i=0}^{n}(P_i' - P_i) \qquad (3.34)$$

in which $TotBM$ is the total blur measurement composed by the summatory of edges width. The edge width is $(P_i' - P_i)$, i is the edge located, P defines the start position, while the local minimum P' corresponds to the end position.

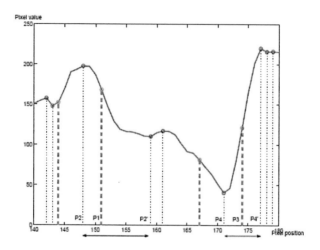

Figure 3.5: Example of Detection of Vertical Edges

3.3.10   Algorithms for Image Quality Assessment

Zhou Wang et al [74] defined a No-Reference (NR) quality measurement algorithm for JPEG compressed images. The NR algorithm first examines the blurring and blocking effects transforming the signal into the frequency domain. The blurring and blocking are calculated horizontally and vertically, the blockiness is estimated as the average differences across block boundaries. Blurring is calculated measuring the reduction of signal activity and measuring the zero-crossing (ZC) rate. The quality assessment model works with parameters that must be estimated with subjective data from the images to be evaluated. Another quality index developed by Zhou Wang et al is the *Universal Objective Image Quality Index* [73]. This index pretends to substitute the error summation methods like mean squared error (MSE), peak signal to noise ratio (PSNR), root mean squared error (RMSE), mean absolute error (MAE) and signal to noise ratio (SNR). The index is designed by modeling any image distortion as a combination of three factors: loss of correlation, luminance distortion and contrast distortion. The index is the result of the comparison of the three factors of two images, the original and the tested image.

3.4   Summary

In this chapter different definitions of the concept quality are presented, for example:

- Quality is an inherent or distinguishing characteristic [9]

- Quality is the conformance of requirements [12]

- Quality is the degree by the series of characteristics in which it must comply with the required specifications [24]

In section 3.1.4 an explanation of subjective scales based on visual analog scale or adjectival scales for quality that can be assigned to an evaluated object are presented. The background of biometrics e.g. concept description and biometrics' classification is presented in section 3.2. In section 3.3 different concepts of image quality established for different authors are described. It is explained the different image quality attributes considered for each author and an explanation of different methods of image quality measurement and the algorithms for image quality assessment are also included.

Chapter 4

Analysis of Conformance Sentences

Conformance sentences represent the quality indicators to be accomplished. In this Chapter the standards in which the quality conformance of this work is based are analyzed. One is the document ICAO "Biometrics Deployment of Machine Readable Travel Documents" specifications [48] and the other is the "ISO/IEC 19794-5 Face Image Data Interchange" [4]. The quality requirements are described in pure text (in natural language). The principal problem is that, basically, natural languages are systems for describing perceptions, and such are intrinsically imprecise in ways that put them beyond the reach of bivalent logic. Closely related to the problem of natural language understanding is the problem of mechanization of reasoning is precisation of meaning [72].

Every sentence that conforms the text of the documents was analyzed, the conformance sentences were abstracted in different phases, they were grouped for common characteristics obtaining for each of the different possible measures or variables that can be measured.

4.1 Standards for the Determination of Facial Image Quality

The documents from international standards related to facial image attributes such as ICAO "Biometrics Deployment of Machine Readable Travel Documents" specifications [48], including it's annexes: "Annex A. Photograph Guidelines", "Annex B. Facial Image Size Study 1", "Annex C. Facial Image Size Study 2", "Annex D Face Image Data Interchange" better known as "ISO/IEC CD 19794-5"[4] were analyzed. As an attribute a property is considered that can be ascribed to a digital passport photograph. The attributes here referred are obtained from the analysis of the standards mentioned. The previous results of the analysis are summarized in Table 4.1; the first column includes the attributes identified and classified according to common characteristics and correlation in the quality perception. The second and third column contain the requirement sentences related to the attribute identified and the fourth column describes restrictions or constraints and/or comments associated with the attribute. In this table the requirements are classified by features of the face image. There are seven components to consider: hair, head, face, eyes region, eye (left or right), mouth and shoulder. For each feature there are given two basic requirements and one special comment with more details of the specifications is included. This table can be used as guide for photographers who want to take photographs with the ICAO specifications or by people in general who want to gain an overview of that document.

Table 4.1: Photograph Taking Guidelines for Travel Documents

Attribute	Requirement 1	Requirement 2	Comment
Hair	without hair	with hair from different hair color	for persons with voluminous hair the specified dimension of the image must reflect the entire face whereby the hair volume may be reflected
Head	without headgear	with headgear (allowed just for religious reasons)	for persons who wear headgear, the face region (from chin to forehead) must be visible
Face	without make-up, without piercing	with make-up, with piercing	no under or overexposure, no covers on the face, neutral face expression (no smile, both eyes normally opened, mouth closed), line of vision directly to the camera
Eyes region	without eyeglasses (of persons with different eye colors)	with eyeglasses (of persons with different eye colors)	for eyeglasses the eyeglass frame may not cover the eyes, no reflections on eyeglass lenses, pupil and iris must be recognizable, no perceptible distortions (e.g. fish eye effect), no "red eye" effect
Eye (left or right)	no eye flap (of persons with different eye colors)	with eye flap (of persons with different eye colors)	Pupil and iris of the right eye must be recognizable, no perceptible distortions, no "red eye" effect
Mouth	without beard	with beard (upper lip beard, chin and/or cheek beard)	the mouth must be closed
Shoulders			shoulders must be visible

The requirements established on the ISO/IEC 19794-5 [4] were analyzed and grouped according to the main topic of every requirement. Figure 4.1 represents a classification scheme of the biometric content quality requirements. The intention of this classification is to enable understanding through relationships between requirements and to allow a clear understanding, i.e. which of them have a direct influence on how good a digital passport photograph is according to the conformance requirements.

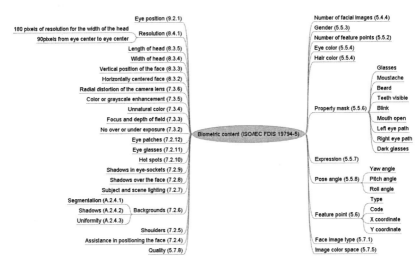

Figure 4.1: Biometric Content Requirements of the ISO/IEC 19794-5

4.2 Achto Cualli: A Method for the Extraction of Conformance Requirements

The evaluation of of quality conditions for passport photographs' feasibility, the conformance requirements that shall be accomplished were analysed in a low level. Conformance requirements are the expressions that convey the criteria to be fulfilled in an implementation of a specification of quality. The conformance requirements are stated in a conformance clause or statement within the specification. This section describes a method called *Achto Cualli*[1] which was created by the author for a systematic extraction of the information that describes the purpose and scope of a conformance clause and the associated issues that a conformance clause shall or may address.

The *Achto Cualli* method was created as the result of the previous Chapters, for example the literature consulted for Chapter 3 related to quality in a general meaning. According to the definition specified in [9] a method is the description of a systematic way in doing something. The *Achto Cualli* method is composed of the following precepts:

1. **Identification of conformance clauses**. The conformance clauses must be identified. They must be translated into short sentences and grouped by common characteristics; each group is called a comprehension set and should have the name of the grouping characteristic. The graphical representation of the relations such as unions or intersec-

---

[1]Achto means firstly, Cualli means the best, in Nahuatl an ancient mexican language. The whole meaning is: firstly the best

tions between sets must be drawn. Logic sentences of relations between sets can be helpful for a better understanding of the conformance clauses, these sentences show the dependence between requirements and a clearly identification of sets and elements that conform to the quality expected.

2. **Identification of requirements' rules, laws, standards or politics related**. The requirements rules, laws, standards or politics related for all groups defined in the first precept are the constraints which control the results of conformance requirements. It is important to specify in this part of the analysis which requirements can be reached and how.

3. **Qualification of requirements**. A weight or numerical scale of each requirement according to the impact degree in the conformance requirements must be assigned.

4. **Integration of fulfillment of requirements into an algorithm**. An algorithm to integrate the conformance requirements has to be programmed using some technology to test the results with the first precept to evaluate if the produced results are valid according to the expected results.

This section is intended for the developers of quality specifications to help enabling them to develop conformance requirements within their specification and to create testable and unambiguous quality specifications. The implementation that conforms to this method shall:

- Contain a list of conformance clauses

- Address all attributes of each conformance clause

- Indicate the applicability and means for achieving conformance to each attribute

- Examine the conformance clauses

- Determine if each clause is applicable

- Define the conformance requirements for applicable items

Each clause shall be clearly identifiable and the identified attribute must be quantifiable. A judgment if a conformance clause can be measured is obtained using the *Achto Cualli* method. In the next subsections the implementation of this method is detailed.

4.2.1   Identification of Conformance Clauses

The identification of conformance requirements is a procedure by which one ascribes the qualities or characteristics, referred in this thesis as attributes related to face image quality specified in the international standards previously mentioned. The identification of conformance requirements phase implies:

- Careful reading of a requirement

- Extraction of a short sentence for every requirement

- Grouping the sentences by common characteristics, calling each group "comprehension set", which should have the name of the grouping characteristic

- Drawing a diagram which shows all possible intersections and unions between requirements and a clear identification of sets and elements that conform to the quality expected

4.2.2 ICAO Requirements Annex A. Photograph Guidelines

In the ICAO document [48] the requirements are specified assuming the photograph is printed and scanned; "For face images, an ICAO-standard size photograph color-scanned at 300dpi results in an image with approximately 90 pixels between the eyes and a size of approximately 643K (kilobytes). This can be reduced to 112K (kilobytes) with very minimal compression". The conformance sentences extracted belong to different types of requirements and the specifications of each descriptive element are presented in the following sections.

4.2.2.1 Photograph Requirements

As photograph requirements are included all the conformance criteria whose main subject is the photograph in conjunction with photograph technical requirements.

1. Must be not older than 6 months

2. Must be 35-40mm in width

3. Must be in sharp focus and clear

4. Must show the natural individual's skin tone

5. Must have the appropriate brightness

6. Must have the appropriate contrast

7. Must be color neutral

8. Must be taken with a plain light-colored background

9. Must be taken with uniform lighting

10. Must not show shadows or flash reflections on the face

11. Must not show red eye

4.2.2.2 Individual's Face Requirements

Conformance sentences related to the individual's face are included in this section.

1. Must show the individual's face alone with a neutral expression

2. Must show the individual's face with mouth closed

3. The face must take up to 70-80% of the photograph

4. The individual's look must be totally directed to the camera

5. The individual's eyes must be open and clearly visible no hair across the eyes

6. The individual's facing square onto the camera, not looking over one shoulder (portrait style) or tilted, and showing both edges of the face clearly

7. Head coverings are not permitted except for religious reasons, but the facial features from bottom of chin to top of forehead and both edges of the face must be clearly shown

4.2.2.3   Lenses

1. The photograph must show the individual's eyes clearly with no flash reflection of the glasses and not tinted lenses; heavy frames have to be avoided if it is possible lighter framed glasses, the frames must not cover any part of the eyes.

4.2.3   ICAO Requirements Annex B. Face Image Size Study #1

This annex encodes the quality requirements related to the face image.

1. The JPEG sequential baseline mode of operation and encoded in the JFIF file format, the JPEG-2000 Part-1 Code Stream Format and encoded in the JP2 file format

2. The maximum allowed amounts of compression for full images to be such that 1mm x 1mm features can be discerned.

4.2.4   ICAO Requirements Annex C. Facial Image Size Study #2

This annex refers to relevant image formats that could be used to store face images.

1. The current standard for storing photographs is JPEG, but the tendency is to use JPEG2000 because of its compression characteristics and because it includes new capabilities

2. The most common lossless compression is the GIF, there are two other formats such as PNG which tends to be more frequently used, and BMP commonly used in MS Windows

4.2.5   ICAO Requirements Annex D. Face Image Data Interchange (ISO /IEC 19794-5)

This annex is better known as a ISO ISO /IEC 19794-5 [47]. It contains specifications of record format for storing, recording, and transmitting the information from one or more face images within a CBEFF data structure. The scene constraints of the face images, photographic

properties of the facial images and digital image attributes of the face images are also specified. Following the objective of this work, this part of the document surveys the clauses related
to the face image quality metrics such as the background, head position, the state of the eyes
and mouth, etc.

4.2.5.1 Photograph Attributes

1. Background

   (a) Segmentation. The boundary between the head and the background should be
   clearly identifiable about the entire subject (very large volume hair excepted)

   (b) Shadows. There should be no shadows visible on the background behind the face
   image.

   (c) Uniformity. The background should be plain, and shall not contain texture like
   lines or curves that could cause computer face finding algorithms to become con-
   fused.

   (d) Assistance in positioning the face. In any case will any other face be captured
   in the Frontal image. Therefore the background should be a uniform color or a
   single color pattern with gradual changes from light to dark luminosity in a single
   direction;

2. Head

   (a) Pose angle. Shall be less than +/- 5 degrees

      i. Yaw angle. If the pose angle is not specified, the value of BY shall be 0
      ii. Pitch angle. If the pose angle is not specified, the value of BP shall be 0
      iii. Roll angle. If the pose angle is not specified, the value of BR shall be 0

   (b) Width of head. In order to assure that the entire face is visible on the image, the
   minimum image width shall be specified by the (Image width : Head width = A :
   CC) ratio of 7 : 5(A : CC 1.4).

   (c) Length of head. In order to assure that the entire face is visible on the image,
   the minimum image height shall be specified by requiring that the crown to chin
   portion of the full frontal image pose shall be no more than 80% of the vertical
   length of the image

3. Shoulders
   Shoulders shall be square to the camera. Portrait style photographs where the individual
   is looking over the shoulder are not acceptable

4. Face

   (a) Number of face images. Normally, more than one face on a facial image is unacceptable. But there is no request in the standard document.

(b) Shadows over the face. The region of the face, from the crown to the base of the chin, and from the ear-to-ear, shall be clearly visible and free of shadows. Special care shall be taken in cases when veils, scarves or headdresses cannot be removed for religious reasons. To ensure these coverings do not obscure any facial features and do not generate shadow; in all other cases head coverings shall be absent.

(c) Hot spots. Care shall be taken to avoid "hot spots", bright areas of light shining into the face.

(d) Horizontally centered face. The approximate horizontal midpoints of the mouth and of the bridge of the nose shall lie on an imaginary vertical line positioned at the horizontal center of the image.

(e) Vertical position of the face. The vertical distance from the bottom edge of the image of an imaginary horizontal line passing through the center of the eyes shall be between 50% and 70% of the total vertical length of the image.

5. Eyes Region

(a) Eye glasses. Glasses shall be clear glass and transparent so the eye pupils and irises are clearly visible. Permanently tinted glasses or sunglasses are acceptable only for medical reasons. Care shall be taken that the glasses frames do not obscure the eyes. There shall be no lighting artifacts or flash reflections on glasses.

(b) Shadows in eye-sockets. There shall be no dark shadows in the eye-sockets due to brow; the iris and pupil of the eyes shall be clearly visible.

(c) Eye patches. The wearing of eye patches is allowed only for medical reasons.

(d) Glasses/Dark glasses. Acceptable only for medical reason.

(e) Blink. A face image with blink will indicate non-compliance with the frontal, full frontal, and taken image types.

6. Mouth

(a) Mouth open. Is not acceptable.

(b) Teeth visible. Is not acceptable.

7. Expression. The expression should be neutral.

8. Others

(a) Subject and scene lighting. Lighting shall be equally distributed on the face.

(b) No over or under exposure. For each patch of skin on the person's face, the gradations in textures shall be clearly visible.

(c) Focus and depth of field. The subject's captured image shall always be in focus from nose to ears and chin to crown. All images will have sufficient depth of focus to maintain greater than two millimeter resolution on the subject's facial features at time of capture; Radial distortion of the camera lenses is not allowed.

(d) Unnatural color. Unnaturally colored lighting like yellow, red, etc. is not allowed;
Color or gray scale enhancement, a process that overexposes or under-develops a
color or grayscale image for purposes of beauty enhancement or artistic pleasure
is not allowed.

(e) Redeye. Is not acceptable.

(f) Resolution at least 180 pixels of resolution for the width of the head, or roughly
90 pixels from eye center to eye center

(g) File type should be in a compressed format such as JPEG2000.

4.2.6 Relations between Requirements of ICAO MRTD

The model *Achto Cualli* specifies to draw relation diagrams to get a better understanding of
the requirements' specifications and their union or intersections. This diagram was created
and is presented in Figure 4.2, the elements of each set of requirements are shown. The
diagram contains four sets which correspond to each annex of the ICAO document. They are
explained in the next part.

4.2.6.1 Annex A

The specifications of Annex A are in blue color and Table 4.2 contains the notation of sets of
attributes grouped by common characteristics. In Annex A "Photograph Guidelines" there are
three sets of requirements for the meaning of notation see Table 4.2:

1. Photograph requirements (A1, A2, A3, A4, A5, A6, A7, A8, A9 and A10)

2. Individual's face requirements (A11, A12, A13, A14, A15, A16, A17)

3. Lenses (A18)

4.2.6.2 Annex B

In Annex B "Face Image Size Study #1" there are two sets of requirements related to encoding
of a digital face image. In Figure 4.2 they are shown in color lilac. For the meaning of
notation, see Table 4.3 the sets founded in Annex B are:

1. Format (B1).

2. Compression (B2).

4.2.6.3 Annex C

In Annex C "Facial Image Study #2" there are two sets of requirements related to relevant
formats that could be used to store digital face image. In Figure 4.2 they are shown in yellow
color. For the meaning of notation, see Table 4.4 the sets founded in Annex C are:

1. Format (C1)

2. Compression (C2)

Table 4.2: Notation of the Set of Attributes of Annex A "Photograph Guidelines"

Notation		Grouping Characteristic	Attributes Description
A1	Antiquity	Photograph	must be no more than 6 months old
A2	Size	Photograph	must be 35-40mm in width
A3	Focus	Photograph	must be in sharp focus and clear
A4	Dermis	Photograph	must show the natural individual's skin tone
A5	Brightness	Photograph	must have the appropriate brightness
A6	Contrast	Photograph	must have the appropriate contrast
A7	Color	Photograph	must be color neutral
A8	Background	Photograph	must be taken with a plain light-colored background
A9	Lighting	Photograph	must be taken with uniform lighting
A10	Redeye	Photograph	must not show red eye
A11	Expression	Individual's face	must show individual's face alone with a neutral expression
A12	Mouth	Individual's face	must show individual's face with mouth closed
A13	Percentage	Individual's face	the face must takes up to 70 - 80 %
A14	Looking	Individual's face	the direction of individual's view must look directly at the camera
A15	Eyes	Individual's face	the individual's eyes must be open and clearly visible -no hair across the eyes
A16	Facing	Individual's face	the individual's facing square on to the camera, not looking over one shoulder (portrait style) or tilted, and slowing both edges of the face clearly
A17	Head	Individual's face	head coverings are not permitted except for religious reasons, but the facial features from bottom of chin to top of forehead and both edges of your face must clearly be shown
A18	Lenses	Individual's face	the photograph must show individual's eyes clearly with no flash reflection off the glasses and not tinted lenses; avoid heavy frames if it is possible wear lighter framed glasses, the frames must not cover any part of the eyes.

Table 4.3: Notation of the Set of Attributes of Annex B "Facial Image Size Study #1"

Notation	Grouping Characteristic	Attributes Description
B1. Format	File format	the JPEG sequential baseline mode of operation and encoded in the JFIF file format, the JPEG-2000 Part-1 Code Stream Format and encoded in the JP2 file format
B2. Compression	File Compression	the maximum allowed amounts of compression for full images to be such that 1mm x 1mm features can be discerned

Table 4.4: Notation of the Set of Attributes of Annex C "Facial Image Size Study #2"

Notation	Grouping Characteristic	Attributes Description
C1. Format	file format	the current standard for storing photographs is JPEG, but the tendency is to use JPEG2000 because it is more powerful and includes new capabilities.
C2. Compression	file Compression	the most common lossless compression is the GIF, but the tendency is to use PNG because is more powerful and patent free, BMP is commonly used in MS Windows.

4.2.6.4   Annex D

In Annex D "Face Image Data Interchange" (ISO/IEC CD 19794-5) there are three sets of requirements related to face image format and computer automated face identification (called in this work biometric content). In Figure 4.2 they are shown in green color, for the meaning of notation, see Table 4.5 the sets founded in Annex D are:

1. Background (D1)

2. Head (D2)

3. Shoulder (D3)

4. Face (D4)

5. Eyes Region (D5)

6. Mouth (D6)

7. Expression (D2)

8. Lighting (D8)

9. Exposure (D9)

10. Focus (D10)

11. Color (D11)

12. Red eye (D12)

13. Resolution (D13)

14. File (D14)

The relations identified between requirements of all Annexes (A, B, C and D) are eighteen, the first sixteen are simple relations between sets but the last two are compound relations: it means that they are relations between sets and other relations. The relations detected are: R1 = (A3,D10), R2 = (R4,D4), R3 = (A7,D11), R4 = (A8,D1), R5 = (A9,D8), R6 = (A10,D12), R7 = (A11,D7), R8 = (A12,D6), R9 = (A14,D5), R10 = (A15,D5), R11 = (A16,D3), R12 = (A16,D4), R13 = (A17,D2), R14 = (A18,D5), R15 = (B1,C1), R16 = (B2,C2), R17 = (D14,R15), R18 = (D14, R16).

R1 to R16 are single relations, R17 and R18 are compound relations. It means that results from R15 and R16 determine the results of R17 and R18. All relations mentioned before show that almost all the specifications of Annex A and D are the same, but presented in different ways. This relations and the isolated elements shown in Figure 4.2 can be translated as the absolute requirements to fulfill. Translating the absolute requirements in natural language they can be expressed as:

- A1 = Photograph must be no more than 6 months old

- A2 = Photograph must be 35-40mm in width

- A5 = Photograph must have the appropriate brightness

- A6 = Photograph must have the appropriate contrast

- A13 = The face must take up to 70 - 80% of the photograph

- A18 = The photograph must show individual's eyes clearly with no flash reflection on the glasses and not tinted lenses; avoid heavy frames, if it is possible wear lighter framed glasses, the frames must not cover any part of the eyes

Table 4.5: Notation of the Set of Attributes of Annex D "Face Image Data Interchange"

	Notation	Grouping Characteristic	Attributes Description
D1	Background	Photograph	this attribute is multidimensional, it has four dimensions: 1. Segmentation; 2. Shadows; 3. Uniformity; 4. Assistance
D2	Head	Individual's face	this attribute is multi-multidimensional, it has three dimensions and each dimension has more than one other dimension: 1. Pose angle; 1.1. Yaw angle; 1.2. Pitch angle; 1.3. Roll angle
D3	Shoulders	Individual's face	shoulders shall be square to the camera in straight frontal position
D4	Face	Individual's face	this attribute has five dimensions: 1. Number of face images; 2. Shadows over the face; 3. Hot spots; 4. Horizontally Centered Face; 5. Vertical position of the face.
D5	Eyes Region	Individual's Face	this attribute is multidimensional it has five dimensions: 1. Eye glasses; 2. Shadows in Eye-sockets; 3. Eye patch; 4. Glasses/Dark glasses; 5. Blink
D6	Mouth	Individual's Face	this attribute has two dimensions: 1. Mouth open is not acceptable; 2. Teeth visibility is not acceptable
D7	Expression	Individual's Face	just neutral expression is acceptable
D8	Lighting	Photograph	must be taken with uniform lighting
D9	Exposure	Photograph	must not be over or under exposure
D10	Focus	Photograph	the individual's frontal face image should be always in focus
D11	Color	Photograph	it is just allowed naturally colored image
D12	Red Eye	Photograph	the red eye effect is not allowed
D13	Resolution	Photograph	at least 180 pixels of resolution for the width of the head or roughly 90 pixels from eye center to eye center
D14	File	Data file	the file type should be in a compressed format such as JPEG2000

- R1 = Photograph must be in sharp focus and clear

- R2 = Photograph must show the natural individual's skin tone; the number of face images should be saved; avoid shadows over the face, avoid hot spots, face should be centered in the horizontal position, vertical position of the face shall be between 50% and 70% of the total vertical length of the image

- R3 = Photograph must be color neutral

- R4 = Photograph must be taken with a plain light colored background

- R5 = Photograph must be taken with uniform lighting

- R6 = Photograph must not show red eyes

- R7 = It shall be one individual's face with a neutral expression

- R8 = Individual's face must have the mouth closed

- R9 = Individual's view must look directly at the camera

- R10 = Individual's eyes must be open and clearly visible with no hair across the eyes

- R11 = Individual's facing square on to the camera, not looking over the shoulder or tilted, and slowing both edges of the face clearly

- R12 = Individual's facing square on to the camera, not looking over the shoulder or tilted, and slowing both edges of the face clearly and avoid shadows over the face, avoid hot spots, face should be centered in the horizontal position, vertical position of the face shall be between 50% and 70% of the total vertical length of the image

- R13 = Head coverings are not permitted except for religious reasons, but the facial features from bottom of chin to top of forehead and both edges of the face must be clearly shown and individual's face pose angle shall be less than +/- 5 degree it should be take into consideration yaw angle, pitch angle and roll angle

- R14 = Individual's eyes clearly with no flash reflection on the glasses and not tinted lenses; avoid heavy frames, if it is possible wear lighter framed glasses, the frames must not cover any part of the eyes

- R15 = File format must be JPEG-2000

- R16 = File compression maximum allowed amounts compression for full images to be such that 1mm x 1mm features can be discerned

- R17 = The file type must be in compressed format such as JPEG2000

- R18 = The file type must be in compressed format such as JPEG2000 which maximum allowed amounts compression for full images to be such that 1mm x 1mm features can be discerned

In Figure 4.2 it can be recognized that A5 and A6 are the only requirements implicitly referred in the four Annexes; there are redundant requirements in the first list obtained. Comparing the specifications from Annex D and Annex A, it can be inferred that: Annex D complements Annex A, Annex B and Annex C are redundant, the ICAO document [48] can be reduced and organized into two Annexes. The first should have the graphical photo requirements (Annex A content) integrating the technical explanation about them (Annex D content), the second one should have all the physical data file requirements and the explanation of some real examples using the specifications.

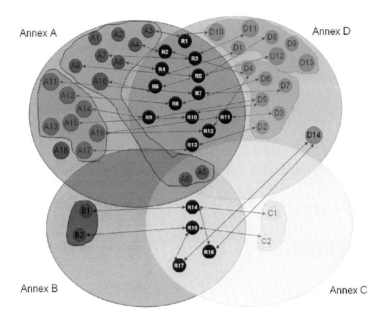

Figure 4.2: Diagram of Relationships between Annex A, Annex B Annex C and Annex D of ICAO MRTD

4.3   Identifying Requirement Rules

The detection of requirements rules, laws, standards or politics related, is a procedure where the constraints that will control the results of conformance requirements for all groups are determined. The importance of this procedure lies in the specification of which requirements can be reached and how. The normative frame is referred for every group of requirements, they are three groups: G1. Photograph requirements; G2. Individual's face requirements and G3. Data file requirements. The following normative requirements contain provisions, which through reference in this text constitute provisions of this document. At the time of publications, the editions indicated below were valid. All standards are subject to revision and parties to agreements based on this document are encouraged to investigate the possibility of applying the most recent editions of the standards indicated previously.

- G1 = {A1, A2, A5, A6, A13, A18, R1, R2, R3, R4, R5, R6}

- G2 = {R7, R8, R9, R10, R11, R12, R13, R14}

- G3 = {R15, R16, R17, R18}

Table 4.6 shows the normative frame for the requirements groups specified before.

Table 4.6: Requirements and Normative Frame

Notation	Requirement type	Rules related
G1	Photograph	ISO 10526:1999/CIE S005/E-1998, CIE Standard Illuminants for Colorimetry, PIMA 7667:2001, Photography - electronic Still Picture Imaging - Extended sRGB Color Encoding - e - sRGB, ICC 1:2001-12, File Format for Color Profiles
G2	Individual's face	New Orleans Resolution March 2003
G3	Data file format	ISO/IEC 19785 Biometric data interchange formats, ISO/IEC 19794-1 Biometric data interchange, ISO/IEC 10918, Digital Compression and Coding of Continuous-tone Still Images, ISO/IEC15444 JPEG2000 Image Coding System

4.4 Conformance Requirements

After the analysis of the requirements the attributes are reorganized; they are segmented into three main groups of requirements, the classification obeys a logic process from the scenario preparation to take a photo to the analysis of each component of the face of an individual. A general classification is the following:

- Photograph requirements. Connote the previous preparation of the scenario to be used; this accomplish the requirements of background uniformity, color, type, reflection and illumination of the scene.

- Image requirements. Include all attributes that have the main influence in the perception, this criteria considers those attributes that have a big impact in visual perception such as brightness and contrast which are common requirements specified in all ICAO Annexes previously mentioned.

- Biometric content. The classification of elements in this group obeys the specifications of head pose angle, face features and shoulders visibility and position.

A matrix called *Achto Cualli Matrix* for each main group of requirements is generated as result of applying this method. Every matrix includes three columns, the first column corresponds to the attribute identifier, the second column corresponds to the name of the attribute, the third column corresponds to a specification that defines the requirements, criteria, or conditions that shall be satisfied by an implementation in order to claim conformance. The conformance clause identifies what must conform and how conformance can be met. The first matrix presented in Table 4.7 contains specifications of photograph requirements, this table facilitates consistent application of conformance for the process of taking the photographs within a specification and promotes interoperability and open interchange between photograph and individual. Table 4.8 represents the second matrix for image requirements, an objective of this table is to provide clear and unambiguous statements for each attribute identified, so that the reader knows what is required in order to claim conformance and what is optional. The third Table 4.9 shows the biometric requirements identified. A class of biometric attributes may consist of several integrated face features rather than a single feature (e.g., eye). Conformance may be defined in terms of the integrated features (all the face) and/or for each attribute. Any restrictions or constraints on the number or types of components that make up the "subject of a conformance claim" shall be specified.

They are in total twenty seven attributes identified from which fourteen are photograph requirements, five are image attributes and seven are biometric attributes.

4.5   Summary

In this chapter the first two precepts were developed. A matrix called *Achto Cualli matrix* for every main group of requirements was generated as result of applying this method. Every matrix includes three columns, the first column corresponds to the attribute identificator, the second column corresponds to the name of the attribute and the third column corresponds to the conformance requirement sentence or sentences. The first matrix presented contains specifications of photograph requirements. The second matrix contains specifications for image requirements, the third shows the biometric requirements identified. Every *Achto Cualli matrix* is useful for a systematic identification of the specified requirements and the constraints that every attribute must accomplish.

The specification of conformance requirements may differentiate conformance claims by designating different conformance degrees in order to apply and categorize requirements according to levels or to indicate the permissibility of extensions. A precedence order of evaluation of attributes shall be defined for every group of requirements.

Table 4.7: Achto Cualli Matrix of Photograph Requirements

ID	Attribute	Constraint
AOF	Antiquity	must be no more than 6 months old
SPH	Size	must be 35-40mm in width-high
FOS	Focus	must be in sharp focus and clear
LGS	Lighting Scene	must be taken with uniform lighting, must not show shadows
SKT	Dermis	must show the natural individual's skin tone
BGD	Background	must be taken with a plain light-colored background
EYS	Eyes	the individual's eyes must be open and clearly visible -no hair across the eyes
FCG	Facing	individual's facing square on to the camera, not looking over one shoulder (portrait style) or tilted, and showing both edges of the face clearly
HCV	Head	head coverings are not permitted except for religious reasons, but the facial features from bottom of chin to top of forehead and both edges of individual's face must be clearly shown
PRG	Percentage	the face must takes up 70-80 % of the photograph
EXP	Exposure	must not be over or under exposure
EXS	Expression	must show the individual's face alone with neutral expression
MCD	Mouth	must show the individual's face with mouth closed
NFR	No Flash Reflection	There shall be no lighting artifacts or flash reflections on glasses

Table 4.8: Achto Cualli Matrix of Image Requirements

ID	Attribute	Constraint
BNS	Brightness	must have the appropriate brightness
CST	Contrast	must have the appropriate contrast
CLR	Color	must be color neutral
NRE	Red eye	must not show red eye
FLT	File	the file type should be in a compressed format such as JPEG2000

Table 4.9: Achto Cualli Matrix of Biometric Requirements

ID	Attribute	Constraint
APA	Head pose angle	the individual's pose angle should be less than +/- 5 degree
WAH	Width of head	the head must be greater than 5/7 of width of image
LOH	Length of head	must be no more than 80% of the vertical length
NRF	Number of faces	only one is accepted
HCF	Horizontally centered face	the face should lies on the vertical line and horizontal center
VP	Vertical position	the vertical position of the face should be between 50% and 70%
RSL	Resolution	at least 180 pixels of resolution for the width of the head
DCE	Distance between center of both eyes	roughly 90 pixels from eye center to eye center

Chapter 5

Categorization of Conformance Requirements Based on an International Survey

The categorization of requirements is the ordering of conformance requirements into groups or sets on the basis of their common characteristics. This new categorization has as basisis three criteria: photograph, image and biometric content. Photograph criteria imply the previous preparation of the scenario to be used. The requirements specified are: background uniformity, color, type, reflection and illumination of the scene. The image criteria have the main influence on the quality perception. This criterion considers those attributes that have a big impact in visual perception such as brightness and contrast that are common requirements specified in all ICAO Annexes mentioned in Chapter 4. Biometric content criterion obey the specifications of head pose angle, width of head, length of head, number of faces, horizontally centered face, vertical position and resolution. An attribute must be qualified to evaluate its accomplishment of the standard´s requirement related. In the analysis and design phase of the attributes qualification, some problems to assign a precedence and relevance of attributes of a passport photo were detected. For example knowing which attributes are most important: resolution or eyes visibility, or for example head pose angle or lighting. Like those questions arise some others related to the rest of the attributes found. Assigning priorities or precedences arbitrarily for an attribute can influence the results of a quality metric.

In a first attempt to order the attributes a questionnaire was applied to two experts: a biometrics expert and a professional photograph expert. The results obtained were precedence orders of requirements considering numeric relevance and the total quantity of elements of each set of attributes. Numeric relevance is obtained through a questionnaire in which a biometrics expert organized a list of requirements according to a precedence value for each attribute in a biometric importance criteria. A subjective relevance through a qualification assigned by a photograph expert was obtained and a subjective value with the relevance description for each attribute was assigned. The values are assigned according to the impact on the photograph´s visual perception as high, medium and low. Both values, numeric relevance and subjective relevance are useful to arrange the attributes in different forms according to the user criteria. To discover the range of responses likely to occur in the population of interest a survey research is used. This survey is exploratory and is also used to discover and raise new possibilities and dimensions of the population of interest. Exploratory surveys should be used as the basis for developing concepts and methods for more detailed surveys[54]. An exploratory survey like the one used intends to elicit a wide variety of responses from individuals with varying viewpoints in a loosely structured manner as the basis for design of a deeper and specialized survey.

The first approach was to explore the opinion of more experts to gain a robust database for the design of a quality metric for face images. Since the international standards ICAO-MRTD and ISO 19794-5 [48], [4] play an important role in the maturation process of security assurance in many countries, a survey to ask the experts from Germany and from other countries about their opinion and perception of quality, face image quality and the use of both international standards was designed. According to Pinsonneault and Kraemer [54], assessment of survey research methodology might be done from any of three different perspectives:

1. Developing insights into appropriate research methodologies: establish appropriate usage of different methodologies

2. Examining the quality of existing research methodologies: assess the strengths and weaknesses of different methodologies as they apply in the topic of interest

3. Identifying where research is needed: determine areas where the application of specific methodologies would be most insightful

Pinnsoneault defines a survey as "means of gathering information about the characteristics, actions, or opinions of a large group of persons, referred to as a population" [54]. In this survey the population of interest are the user-experts in the fields of research, control, development or management of personal identification documents with a facial image.

5.1 Survey Objective

The survey is conducted for research purposes, it aims to produce quantitative descriptions of some aspects of the studied population. Most answers are scored using the mean opinion score (MOS) scale that uses the mathematical average to obtain a quantitative indicator[66]. Other answers are scored using subjective scales. The main purposes of this survey are

- Evaluation of the perception of the definition of quality in a general sense

- Evaluation of the perception of the face image quality concept

- Identification of a relative state of the art of the relationship between security and the use of ICAO-MRTD and ISO 19794-5 [48], [4] as international standard to control the quality of face images

- Evaluation of the perception, classification, relevance, and precedence of quality requirements specified in ICAO-MRTD and ISO 19794-5 [48], [4]

- Identification of face image working groups around the world. The interest of the identification of face image working groups is for establishing contact with the research community from the same areas of interest.

- Comparison between the opinions of practical and technical user-experts to find convergences and divergences of opinions between both groups.

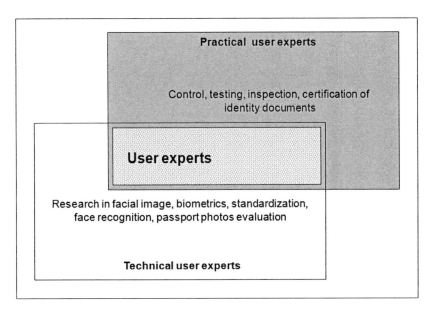

Figure 5.1: 2DFIQ Survey Framework

5.2 Methodology of the Survey

The survey is addressed to persons who have experience in working directly or indirectly with face images. Two kinds of user-experts were identified: *practical user-experts* and *technical user-experts*. In the first group persons were included whose main activities are one or more of the following: control, testing, inspection, certification of identity documents with a face image like passport, visa, driver's license etc. In the second group persons were included who have made research in the fields of digital face images, biometrics, standardization, face recognition, evaluation of passport photographs, IT security, software development etc. The framework of this survey consists of the analysis of results of two basic frames. The first frame is compound of practical user-experts opinions and the second frame is compound of technical user-experts opinion. These frames are characterized by the use of facial images in the daily activities of both groups. Figure 5.1 shows the survey framework design in which the main activities of each group of experts can be included and as common factor the use of facial images for their work.

5.2.1 Specification of Results to be Obtained

According to the objective of the survey, the results planed to be obtained are specified in Table 5.1. The first column shows the variable's name and the second column shows the kind of expected value. Many variables are defined, for example Quality, Face Image Quality, Perception of Quality etc. Since the user-experts perform daily activities controlling identity documents from traveling persons, there is a particular interest in knowing if the control is just administrative or based on safety rules. It is of major interest to evaluate, if the perception of quality requirements of the user-expert-groups is in accordance with the quality definition in the standards. The relevance order of quality attributes refers to the importance the user groups assign to the attributes which allows to compare the results of the groups. Another benefit obtained from this explorative international survey is the identification of research groups dealing with face image quality around the world. As the survey is developed for two kinds of experts, the convergences and divergences of opinions to identify the possibility of criteria unification are also analyzed.

5.3 Obtaining Survey Data

For practical user-experts an on-site survey was supplied. The experts have been visited and the questionnaire were directly applied at their work places. The questionnaires were answered at the following locations: Frankfurt airport at the check-in zone and at the border police as well as at the municipal department for public order in Darmstadt, Germany. For the the technical user-experts the Internet was used for the data collection. They were invited through a personalized email. An on-line survey was designed, directed to contact technical user-experts from different countries within a relatively short time. For this on-line survey a web-based application in a three-layer platform (web and applications server, database server, and a web-browser as client) was created. The technical user-experts group was surveyed through an on-line research strategy using different data sources to obtain the email addresses and professional profiles for example:

- Lists of participants in specialized conferences (Biometrics Quality, Face Recognition)

- Internet search engines such as Google, Yahoo, Altavista, WebCrawler and Windows Live with the keywords face image, face recognition, face research, personal identity, face image standardization, biometrics

- One-to-one referencing: this strategy consisted in asking colleagues or friends to invite other colleagues or friends who possess the user-expert profile to answer the survey

Table 5.1: Results Expected from the Face Image Quality Survey

Result	Description	Value expected
Quality	Definition of quality in a general sense	qualitative: list of terms that compound the quality definition according to user-experts opinion
Face image quality	Definition of face image quality concept	qualitative: list of terms that compound the face image quality definition in compliance to user-experts opinion
Relationship between security and face image control	State of the art of the relationship between security and the use of ICAO-MRTD and ISO 19794-5 [48], [4] as international standard to control the quality of face image	qualitative: list of terms associated with the relationship
Perception of quality requirements	Coincidence of user-experts opinions with the requirements specified in ICAO-MRTD and ISO 19794-5 [48], [4]	quantitative: percentage of coincidences
Precedence order of quality attributes	Classification of quality requirements specified in ICAO-MRTD and ISO 19794-5 [48], [4] in ascendant order in compliance to user-experts opinion	qualitative: list of attributes
Relevance order of quality attributes	Quality attribute occurrence in the user-experts opinion and comments	qualitative: list of attributes
Face image working groups	Identification of face image working groups around the world	qualitative: list of working groups established
Opinion convergence	Opinion convergences between practical and technical user-experts	quantitative: percentage of convergences
Opinion divergence	Opinion divergences between practical and technical user-experts	quantitative: percentage of divergences

5.3.1   Background of the Participants

Survey research is a quantitative method, requiring standardized information about the subjects being stuided. A total of 400 experts from 25 countries was invited, 30 practical user-experts and 370 technical user-experts. The practical user-experts were invited personally in different sessions and work times.

5.3.2   Profiles of Participants

A person to be qualified as expert should cover the requirement of working directly or indirectly with face images in his/her daily activities and the use of some kind of normative document to perform his/her activities. The contacted experts can have one of the following positions in an organization, university or company as shown in Table 5.2:
International standards play an important role in the maturation process of security control in its different variations. In many countries the initiatives to establish a standardized process for the issue of personal identity documents, especially produced for the control of travel documents have been favored and highly prioritized for the last four years. In this survey's section the information of survey responses is presented. In order to compile information of the greater number of potential face image user-experts from different countries, the on-line survey has been addressed to persons from 25 different countries. This demographic information can be a reference guide for detecting the acceptance of the standards referred to the previous section. This section includes the country's name, type of organization, company or university, position, activities related to face images and normative documents used. Most of the technical user-experts are persons who have between one and eleven years of experience working with face images, while the practical user-experts are persons who have experience ranging from two days to fourteen years working in the function of identity documents controller.

5.4   Selected Results of the Survey

5.4.1   Participation in the Survey

A total of 20 persons answered the survey on-site. From persons invited by e-mail to answer the on-line survey, 5 e-mails were answered automatically as out of office messages, 75 e-mails were rejected due to a problem with the e-mail account of the addresses, 175 e-mails were not answered, and 66 persons participated in answering the on-line survey. Table 5.3 shows the distribution of invited and persons who have participated, grouped by countries. This table expresses the grade of responses from each country and the proportion obtained between persons invited and persons who reacted to the survey.

5.4.2   Institutions of the Participants

This survey explores specialists' answers from 59 different institutions. 33.89% of the answers came from universities, 13.55% came from research institutes, 25.42% came from spe-

Table 5.2: User-Experts' Profiles

Candidate's Position 1	Candidate's Position 2
Account Manager	Application Security Architect
Application Security Engineer	Associate Software Engineer
Auditor Cert Security Consultant	Certification & Accreditation Engineer
Channel/Business Development	Check-in Agent
Chief Scientist	Chief Security Officer (CSO)
Compliance Officer	Customer Service
Customer Support	Database Security Architect
Database Security Engineer	Developer
Director of Privacy and Security	Disaster Recovery Coordinator
Forensics Engineer	Identification Document Controller
Incident Handler	Information Assurance Analyst
Information Assurance Engineer	Instructor
Junior Security Analyst	Junior Researcher
Management	Manager
Information Security	Penetration Engineer
Personal Identification Controller	Physical Access Controller
Principal Software Engineer	Privacy Officer
Product Strategist	Quality Assurance Specialist
Regional Channel Manager	Research Engineer
Sales Engineer	Sales Representative
Security Analyst	Security Architect
Security Auditor	Security Consultant
Security Director	Security Engineer
Security Evangelist	Security Product Manager
Security Product Marketing Manager	Security Researcher
Security System Administrator	Senior Product Manager
Senior Researcher	Senior Security Engineer
Senior Software Engineer	Software Engineer
Technical Editor	Technical Marketing Engineer
Technical Support Engineer	Technical Writer
Technology Risk Consultant	Threat Analyst
Training/Awareness Specialist	VP Information Security
VP of Marketing	VP of Regional Sales

Table 5.3: Number of Persons Invited and Having Participate, Grouped by Countries

Country of Origin	Invited Persons	Persons Having Participated
Afghanistan	0	1
Australia	4	0
Austria	6	2
Brazil	5	1
Canada	8	1
Chile	4	1
China	23	4
Croatia	1	2
Denmark	13	4
Finland	12	2
France	3	1
Germany	68	40
Israel	2	0
Italy	5	1
Japan	2	1
Korea	5	0
Mexico	9	1
Netherlands	5	1
Norway	0	1
Singapore	2	0
Slovenia	10	0
Spain	4	1
Sweden	1	0
Switzerland	1	0
Turkey	1	1
United Kingdom	41	5
United Sates of America	165	15
Total	370	86

cialized companies, 20.33% came from government agencies, 3.38% came from airlines, and 3.38% did not answer this question. Figure 5.2 shows the percental distributions of the participants organizations.

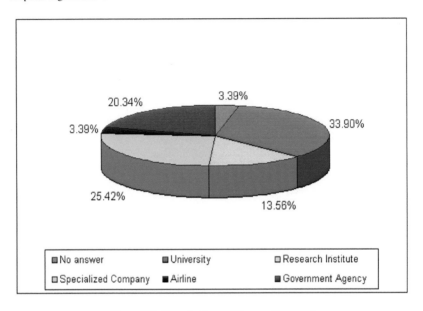

Figure 5.2: Organizations of Persons Surveyed

5.4.3   Positions of Participants

81 persons responded to this question. Table 5.4 shows the distribution of participant's positions. The main percentage obtained came from chief scientists with 16% of participation, the second highest percentage of participation came from check-in agents with 12%. Other positions of participants are e.g.: research engineer, senior researcher, developer, instructor, security researcher, software engineer, account manager, junior researcher, senior software engineer.

5.4.4   Activities Executed by the Experts Surveyed

The main activities performed by the experts surveyed are reflected in the first and second columns of Table 5.5. Most of the activities are related with face recognition and face image quality. Some of the answers obtained reflected attitudes towards: face recognition development, passport control, visa control, personal identification control, research in face detection

Table 5.4: Distribution of Participants, Grouped by Position

Position	%
Chief Scientist	16.04
Check-in Agent	12.34
Research Engineer	11.11
Senior Researcher	8.6
Developer	7.40
Instructor	4.9
Security Researcher	4.9
Software Engineer	4.9
Account Manager	3.7
Junior Researcher	3.7
Senior Software Engineer	3.7
Management	2.46
Personal Identification Controller	2.46
Security Engineer	2.46
Application Security Architect	1.23
Forensics Engineer	1.23
Identification Document Controller	1.23
Manager Information Security	1.23
Principal Software Engineer	1.23
Sales Representative	1.23
Security Analyst	1.23
Security Architect	1.23
Security Consultant	1.23

and recognition, research and development management in face recognition and related files, research in computer vision, research work on face image processing and analysis, research into 2D/3D face recognition, research and standardization of face images and research in integration of identification-based systems.

5.4.5   Use of a Normative Document

The participants were asked to select just one type of normative document used in their daily activities. Three kinds of normative documents were offered: best practices, law-related and standard. For an alternative answer a field was included to fill in an alternative document not listed previously.

Objective. The use of a normative document and the use of ICAO-MRTD and ISO 19794-5 [48], [4] were evaluated.

Result. This question was answered by 81 persons, a total of 77 recognized the use of one of the documents listed to perform the daily activities related to face image quality, while the rest stated to use other types of normative documents. Table 5.7 shows the distribution of type of normative documents segregated by group of participants. Most of the persons that specified as main activity the control of passports, visa or personal identity answered that the control of a face image is based on corporate documents and on experience, not necessarily on an international standard. The participants declared to use the following documents presented in Table 5.6 as normative documents in the performance of their daily activities related to face images.

5.4.6   Definition of Quality by the Participants

The interpretation of the concept "'quality"' involves different meanings. It can be interpreted according to the point of view or according to the requirements to be conformed and the demands of the user. The participants were asked to select a phrase that defines quality best. The purpose of this question is to compare the interpretation of the quality concept from both groups of experts and to identify which concepts can be mixed to form an integrated quality concept considering the opinions of the participants. This section includes the analysis of the use and interpretation of different concepts of quality. Some different definitions of quality in its general concept were included to determine the variations of quality concepts and the most frequently term applied by the user-experts to develop their activities related to face image quality.

Quality Concept. According to the dictionary of English language [9] quality is an inherent or distinguishing characteristic; Philip Crosby, considered as one of the most important authors of the quality revolution in [12], specifies that quality is the conformance of requirements. The best known International Quality Standard: ISO 9000 in its quality definition [24] determines that quality is the degree with that a set of inherent characteristics fulfills requirements. These concepts determine the principle to evaluate how well a face image can accomplish the conformance requirements established by ICAO-MRTD and ISO 19794-5 [48], [4]. Figure 5.3 compares opinions of technical and practical user-experts. It can be estimated that for the majority (39%) of technical user-experts the meaning of Quality is: *an inherent or*

Table 5.5: Activities of Participants

Main Activity 1	Main Activity 2
Face recognition development	Passport control
Visa control	Personal identification control
Research in face detection and recognition	Research and development management in face recognition and related files
Research in computer vision	Research work on face image processing and analysis
Research in neurosciences	Research into 2D/3D face recognition
Research and standardization of face images	Research in integration of identification-based systems
Analysis of face recognition algorithms performance	Analysis of biometrics
ICAO portrait control (ISO quality assessment of face images)	Advising government agencies
Advising the government regarding all questions of facial quality software for passport applications	Development of face recognition systems
Development of biometric software	Development of ID related solutions
Development of projects to evaluate face recognition	Development of projects for automatic image analysis (recognition and detection)
Testing of biometric systems	Exploring image compression effects on face recognition and developing fully compressed domain facial recognition system
Development of standards	Development of modern facial recognition techniques (SVM, recognition by parts as well as common discriminators)
Development for 3D face recognition	Development of projects related to smart cards
Consulting in IT security and biometrics	Development of projects for electronic passport
Implementation of face finding algorithms, face image quality assessment and enhancement	Enrollment and quality assurance

Table 5.6: Normative Documents Used for the Experts' Group

Normative Document
Corporate manual
ICAO and SC37 documents
Papers in the leading academic journals
Laws depending on the country to be visited (check-in agent answer)
ISO/IEC 19794-5
Academic surveys
ISO/IEC 19794-1 and 2
ISO/IEC JTC 1/SC 37 Documents
NIST-ITL-1-2001/2006
Directives of the Federal Ministry
EU directives
ICAO, DIN, ISO
Tutorials published on the world wide web, blogs
Guidelines of the Federal Print Office

Table 5.7: Types of Normative Documents Used, Ordered by Group of Participants

Type of Document	Practical user-experts	Technical user-experts
Best practices	7	6
Law related	7	5
Other document	6	16
Standard	0	30
Total	20	57

distinguishing characteristics property while for the majority(45%) of practical user-experts, Quality means: *fulfilment of legal and regulatory requirements.* As second meaning of quality technical user-experts choose the *conformance of requirements* having 32% of opinions. For practical user-experts the second meaning selected having 30% is the degree or grade of excellence.

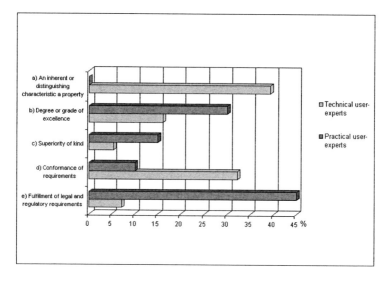

Figure 5.3: Quality Perception of User-Experts

5.4.7 Perception of Face Image Quality

Face Image Quality Perception. The concept of Face Image Quality as the quality concept by itself can be interpreted depending on its use and depending on the normative documents to be used.

Objective. The objective of this question is to compare the results of perception of face image quality from both groups of experts and to identify the used concepts to form an integrated face image quality concept considering the opinion of the participants and the specifications of the ICAO MRTD and ISO 19794-5 [48], [4]. This perception was evaluated asking the participants which of the following sentences describes best a good quality of a face image:

1. The image has a good resolution

2. The face is recognizable

3. The color is neutral

4. The image fulfills the specifications established

5. The image file permits good performance in the software used

These sentences refer to requirements related specifically to face images of the standards mentioned previously and using a quality concept in a general sense.

Result. A total of 76 persons answered this question of which 56 are technical user-experts and 20 are practical user-experts. Figure 5.4 shows a graphic of the results obtained, while Table 5.8 shows the results ordered by a group of experts. The definition *"the image fulfills the specifications"* obtained the majority of selections from both groups of experts. For the practical user-experts the second definition selected is *"the face is recognizable"* while for the technical user-experts the second definition selected is *"the image permits good performance in the software used"*. These variance reflects a difference of interests of both groups of experts. For practical user-experts the priority is to recognize and to control adequately the individual's face in the image, while the technical user-experts are interested in a better performance regardless of the fact whether or not the face is recognizable in the image. Most practical user-experts who participated in the survey have expressed the need for a powerful software which automatically permits the face recognition of a personal identity document.

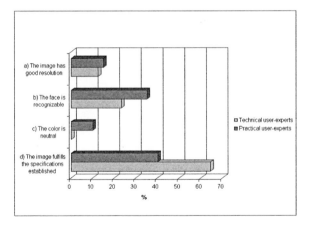

Figure 5.4: Face Image Quality Perception of User-Experts

5.4.8   Digital Face Image Quality Perception

This perception was evaluated based on the requirements specifically related to digital face images prescribed in [4].

Objective. The objective of this question is to evaluate the interpretation of quality of a digital photo. The users were asked to choose among the following statements which one defines best the quality of a digital face image:

Table 5.8: A Face Image Quality Perception of User-Experts

Quality Statement	Practical user-experts (%)	Technical user-experts (%)
1	15	12
2	35	23
3	10	0
4	40	64

Table 5.9: Digital Face Image Quality Perception of User-Experts

Sentence of Quality	Practical user-experts (%)	Technical user-experts (%)
1	25	11
2	30	16
3	0	0
4	35	46
5	10	25

1. The image has a good resolution

2. The face is recognizable

3. The color is neutral

4. The image fulfills the specifications established

5. The image file permits good performance in the software I use

The last sentence was included to assess how important the performance of a software is for each group of experts to evaluate the quality of a face image.

Result. A total of 75 persons answered this question from which 55 are technical user-experts and 20 are practical user-experts. Figure 5.4 shows the graphics of the results obtained, while Table 5.9 shows the results ordered by groups of experts.

For technical user-experts the most important criterion for evaluating the quality of a face image is rated with 46% when the image fulfils the specifications established. This criterion is also the most important one for practical user-experts comming up to 35% of selections. The second one for practical user-experts with 30% is the condition when the face is recognizable, while for technical user-experts it is when the image permits good performance in the software to be used.

From the population surveyed, the same percentage (25%) from each group reflected the different research interests and this divergence of results can be interpreted as the way technical user-experts are conducting their work. It might be interpreted which they are sometimes producing results that do not satisfy the needs of the practical user-experts.

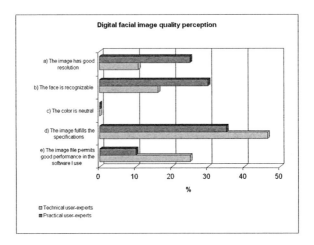

Figure 5.5: Quality Perception of User-Experts

5.4.9 Relevance of Face Image Quality Attributes

In this section the theoretical interpretation of relevance is scrutinized in different ways. First, there have been shown five different groups of requirements extracted from the international standards to the participants. The results are compared between each other; some groups are made up of one type of requirements and others are assembled as a combination of different types of requirements. The following list shows the structure of the groups' requirements:

1. Group A. Photograph Requirements.

   • Size of photograph
   • Antiquity of the photograph
   • Background
   • Neutral expression
   • No flash reflection

2. Group B. Combination of Image and Photograph Requirements.

- Brightness
- Contrast
- No red eye
- Eyes visibility
- Mouth closed

3. Group C. Biometric Attributes

    - Head pose angle
    - Width and length of head
    - Distribution of head over the image
    - Face features are recognizable

4. Group D. Combination of Photograph, Image and Biometric Requirements

    - Background
    - Head pose angle
    - Brightness
    - Contrast
    - Image resolution

5. Group E. Combination of Photograph and Biometric Attributes

    - Eyes visibility
    - Image resolution
    - Head distribution
    - Head pose angle
    - It must show just one face

This first evaluation was made asking to select one of two groups shown in four questions of the survey's questionnaire.

- Group A vs. Group B
- Group C vs. Group D
- Group A vs. Group E

The participants assigned a relevance for every group of photos which is measured as follows: for the on-line survey the order in which an attribute group was selected and saved in the database in real time at the moment when the survey was answered. The precedence was registered in the database. For the on-site survey an order of precedence, assigned by the participants, was indicated. The percentage of selections obtained for each group in each

question was obtained according to the number of votes or selections obtained for each group. The groups were ordered in descendant order according to the percentage obtained for each group.
The relevance assigned by the technical user-experts is ordered as follows:

1. Group C: 71%

2. Group E: 70%

3. Group B: 53%

4. Group A: 46%

5. Group D: 58%

For practical user-experts the relevance is rated as follows:

1. Group B: 65%

2. Group C: 60%

3. Group D and E: 40% each one

4. Group A: 35%

The second evaluation of the relevance of attributes was conducted showing the same attributes together and asking the users to assign a number for their precedences whereas 1 represents the most important requirement and 14 the least important. The attributes are shown in Table 5.10; the first column corresponds to the precedence number, the second contains the attributes shown, the third column contains the order selected by the practical user-experts, and the fourth column contains the order selected by technical user-experts.
The relevance order was obtained from a table of the survey database filled in by user-experts. Every question gained the highest value and corresponding attribute from every relevance number. Figure 5.6 shows the logic flowchart followed to determine the relevance order for every attribute from both groups of experts. The evaluation process begins selecting the question qn in this case $qn = 14$, the quantity of user-experts for attribute is j, n is the total number of relevances to be evaluated, i is the actual relevance in evaluation. The highest relevance value and its corresponding attribute are obtained from column i before being saved. It is validated if there is already a value saved for that attribute, if not the values corresponding to user-expert type, relevance value and attribute name are saved. If there is a value previously saved for that attribute, the next highest value for the next attribute is obtained. Table 5.10 shows the results for the relevances obtained for every attribute and group of experts.
For technical user-experts the most important requirement is *neutral expression* with 34% of votes, the least important requirement is *contrast* with 27% of votes. For practical user-experts with 25% of preferences the most important requirement is *Size of head distribution* while *Size of photography* is the least important having 20% of preferences. The third evaluation of relevance of attributes was conducted showing seven requirements together and asking the participants to assign a number for their precedence where 1 is the most important requirement

Table 5.10: Second Relevance Evaluation of Quality Attributes

Order	Attribute pre-sented	Practical user-experts	Technical user-experts
1	Size of the photo-graph	Size of the head distribution	Neutral expres-sion
2	Antiquity of the photograph	Brightness	No red eye
3	Brightness	Size of the pho-tograph	Size of the head distribution
4	Contrast	Contrast	Background
5	Background	Antiquity of the photograph	Size of the pho-tograph
6	Neutral expression	Neutral expres-sion	Antiquity of the photograph
7	No flash reflection	Horizontally centered face	Vertical posi-tion
8	Size of the head distribution	Width of head	No flash reflec-tion
9	Width of head	Background	Width of head
10	Red eye	Head pose an-gle	Horizontally centered face
11	Head pose angle	No flash reflec-tion	Length of head
12	Horizontally cen-tered face	Vertical posi-tion	Brightness
13	Vertical Position	No red eye	Head pose an-gle
14	Length of head	Size of the pho-tograph	Contrast

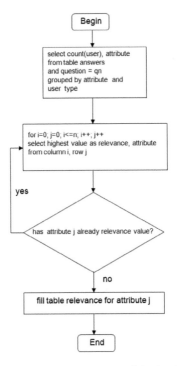

Figure 5.6: Flowchart of Relevance Selection Criteria

and 7 is the least important. The requirements evaluated are presented in Table 5.11. The order of relevance was obtained in the same way as the second evaluation explained above. The logic is shown in Figure 5.6; in this case question $qn = 43$ and $n = 7$. Table 5.11 shows the results of relevances obtained for every attribute and group of experts.

Another approach to evaluate the relevance of attributes was followed by the visual perception test. It consists in asking participants to select the one photo out of a group of five that accomplishes or does not accomplish a specific quality requirement. A total of four groups of photographs were selected for the visual test. In the following paragraphs it will be explained, how the different attributes were evaluated. It shall be emphasized that all the attributes referred to were analyzed and described previously. For more details about the international standards specifications that section might be consulted. The percentages to be presented in this part are the highest values obtained as results for each evaluation.

Group of Photographs Used
For the following evaluations, the first group of photographs shown in Figure 5.7 was used.

Table 5.11: Third Relevance Evaluation of Quality Attributes

Order	Attribute pre-sented	Practical user-experts	Technical user-experts
1	Background	Eyes	Shoulders
2	Mouth	Background	Head
3	Head	Mouth	Hair
4	Hair	Head	Eyes
5	Eyes	Hair	Background
6	Shoulders	Shoulders	Nose
7	Nose	Nose	Mouth

Figure 5.7: First Group of Photographs for Visual Test: Brightness and Contrast

Figure 5.8: Second Group of Photographs for Visual Test: Eyes Region

This group contains five photographs; photograph b) has been altered adding 30% more contrast, and photograph e) has been altered adding 30% more brightness, photograph d) has been included because of the characteristics of eyeglass frames. In every evaluation the results presented are the highest percentages calculated.

Evaluation of Brightness. The first concerned tested requirement is brightness. The participants were asked to select which photo did not reflect an appropriate brightness; the answers given were b) and e). Brightness is related to the luminance of an object, in this case e) is the correct answer. The percentage of correct answers for each user-experts group is:

Figure 5.9: Third Group of Photographs for Visual Test: Face Region

Figure 5.10: Fourth Group of Photographs for Visual Test: Complete Image

- Technical user-experts: 54%

- Practical user-experts: 35%

Evaluation of eyes region: It was asked to select the photograph that does not have good quality within the eyes region. All the photographs are correct. The percentages obtained are:

- Technical user-experts: 74% selected photograph c) which has bad quality because of its reflection on eyeglass lenses.

- Practical user-experts: 35% selected photograph d) because the eyeglass frame was not adequate.

Evaluation of contrast: For this attribute it was asked to select a photograph that does not have an adequate contrast. The correct answers are b) and e)

- Technical user-experts: 48% vote that photograph e) does not have appropriate contrast and 47% considered that photograph b) as the correct answer.

- Practical user-experts: 50% vote that photograph e) does not have appropriate contrast while 35% answered correctly when selecting photograph b)

Evaluation of overexposure: As fourth requirement the participants had to select the photograph with overexposure. The correct answer is e)

- Technical user-experts: 91% mean that photograph e) is overexposed.

- Practical user-experts: 90% have the impression that photograph e) is overexposed.

Evaluation of color neutrality: The understanding of color neutrality was the fifth evaluated requirement. The participants had to select a photograph that is not color neutral. The correct answer is b)

- Technical user-experts: 34% have the impression that photograph b) is not color neutral.

- Practical user-experts: 70% mean that photograph b) is not color neutral.

Evaluation of automatic face recognition understanding: As last evaluation of this group of photographs, it was asked which photograph could possibly complicate the face recognition through a software. The correct answers are b) and e).

- Technical user-experts: 67% of technical user-experts selected photograph e).

- Practical user-experts: 53% of technical user-experts selected photograph e).

Group of photographs used:
For the following evaluation, the second group of photographs shown in Figure 5.8 was used. In this group the photograph d) from the first group was also included because of its characteristics mentioned. Photograph f) was included because the left eye of the individual has a cross-eyed problem and this is one of the exceptions not considered in the standard. Photograph g) was included because the individual is wearing a flap in the right eyes region. The standard permits an eye flap only because of health reasons. If someone is wearing an eye flap, the user-expert must automatically know if the eye flap is used because of health reasons.

Evaluation of line of sight: In this evaluation it was asked to select in which photograph the individual was not looking directly to the camera.

- Technical user-experts: 53% think that photograph f) does not fulfil that requirement

- Practical user-experts: 55% think that photograph f) does not fulfil that requirement

In the comments about this photograph it became obvious, that most of the persons think the photograph was manipulated to obtain the eye effect. Most of participants mentioned it does not fulfill the quality requirement because the person is not looking directly into the camera with both eyes. However it is a real photograph from someone who has a physical problem and it does not mean that the photograph has a bad quality.

Evaluation of eyes visibility:
It was asked to indicate which photograph does not accomplish the sentence *the individual's eyes must be open and clearly visible*. All answers are correct.

- Technical user-experts: 81% answered that photograph g) does not accomplish the requirement except the person uses the patch because of health reasons

- Practical user-experts: 80% answered that photograph g) does not accomplish the requirement except the person uses the patch because of health reasons.

Evaluation of automatic face recognition understanding: As last evaluation with this group of photographs, it was asked which photograph could complicate the face recognition through a software.

- Technical user-experts: 84% selected photograph g)

- Practical user-experts: 65% selected photograph g)

Group of photographs used: For the following evaluations, the third group of photographs shown in Figure 5.9 was used. This group of photographs has a variety of special characteristics; photograph k) is included because of the skin color of the individual, photograph l) is included because of the head cover and skin color of the individual, photograph m) is included because of the hair distribution and color, the piercing and the make-up.

Evaluation of automatic face recognition understanding: The third group included photographs considered as good quality. The participants were asked which photograph would affect the face recognition.

- Technical user-experts: 50% selected photograph k) and 50% selected photograph l)

- Practical user-experts: 51% selected photograph k) and 49% selected photograph l)

Photograph k) has good quality, nevertheless half of all users think that it does not have good quality because the skin color is too dark. A technical user-expert mentioned that *"dark complexions cause problems for some face recognition systems"*. For photograph l), the user-experts think that it does not have good quality because of the head cover.

Group of photographs used: For the following evaluations the fourth group of photographs shown in Figure 5.10 was used. The fourth group is compiled of photographs considered as bad quality because none of them fulfills the requirements specified for eyeglasses reflection, brightness, contrast, facial expression, and head distribution.

Evaluation of automatic face recognition understanding: Participants were asked which photograph would affect the face recognition. All photographs can be valid for a face recognition system, nevertheless they have no good quality because they fail in meeting conformance requirements defined in ICAO-MRTD [48] and ISO 19794-5 [4].

- Technical user-experts: 41% selected photograph p) and 30% selected photograph q)

- Practical user-experts: 35% selected photograph p) and 35% selected photograph t)

The visual evaluation of the requirements shows that the meaning of the specifications of the documents is not clear and that there are some variations related to physical defects of the individual face which should be included in the phrasing of requirements. Many participants assign a photograph a bad quality just because of a physical defect of an individuals eye. Most of the participants assigned another photograph a bad quality because of the individuals skin color. About the evaluated quality scales some of the participants expressed that it would be better to know, under which criteria a photo can be accepted or rejected.

Table 5.12: Organizations with Research Groups in Face Image and/or Biometrics

	Organization	Country		Organization	Country
1	Fujitsu Laboratories	Japan	2	Univ. of Bologna	Italy
3	Nanjing University	China	4	Mitretek Systems	USA
5	University of Sao Paulo	Brazil	6	Bogazi University	Turkey
7	Technical University of Catalunya	Spain	8	Cyberextruder	USA
9	Queen Mary University	UK	10	University of Kent	UK
11	University of California	USA	12	Siemens Austria	Austria
13	Identity Solutions	UK	14	Siemens	USA
15	FBI	USA	16	UNAM	Mexico
17	Bundeskriminalamt	Germany	18	Secunet Security Networks AG	Germany
19	University of Zagreb	Croatia	20	Image Ware System	USA
21	University of Oulu	Finland	22	Aalborg University	Denmark
23	University of Ilinois at Urbana Champaign	USA	24	Mitsubishi Electric Research Laboratories	USA
25	ZGDV	Germany	26	Aalborg University	Denmark
27	Fraunhofer IGD	Germany	28	University of Twente	Netherlands
29	Universidad de Chile	Chile	30	Gjovik University	Norway
31	Steria Mummert Consulting	Germany	32	Carnegie Mellon University	USA
33	Bundesdruckerei	Germany	34	Sagem DS	France
35	Institute of Computing Technology	China			

The scoring obtained to assign a relevance order for the quality attributes evaluated is reflected in Table 5.13, where the most relevant attribute is scored with twentyseven and the lowest relevant attribute is scored with one. Due the answers obtained from the user-experts the most significative attributes scored are the first fifteen.

5.4.10   Research Groups Identified

Another result of the survey is the identification of research groups working with face image and/or in biometrics around the world as presented in Table 5.12.

5.5   Summary

In the analysis and design phase of the attributes qualification, some problems to assign a precedence and relevance of attributes of a passport photo were detected. For example knowing which attribute is most important: resolution or eyes visibility, or for example head pose angle or lighting. Assigning priorities or precedences arbitrarily for an attribute can influence the results of a quality metric. The first approach was to explore the opinion of as many experts as possible to gain a robust database for the design of a quality metric for face images. Since the international standards ICAO-MRTD and ISO 19794-5 [48], [4] play an important role in the maturation process of security assurance in some countries a survey to ask the experts from Germany and from other countries about their opinion and perception of quality, face image quality perception and the use of both international standards was established. Two kinds of user-experts were identified: *practical user-experts* and *technical user-experts*. In the first group persons were included whose main activities are one or more of the following: control, testing, inspection, certification of identity documents with a face image like passport, visa, driver's license etc. In the second group persons were included who have made research in the fields of digital face image, biometrics, standardization, face recognition, passport photos evaluation. IT security, software development, etc. The framework of this survey consists of the analysis of results of two basic frames. The first frame is compound of practical user-experts and the second frame is compound of technical user-experts. These frames are characterized by the use of facial images in the daily activities of both groups of user-experts. The results obtained from the survey are: Definition of quality in a general sense, definition of face image quality concept, relationship between security and face image control, coincidences of user-experts opinions with the requirements specified in ICAO-MRTD and ISO 19794-5 [48], [4], precedence order of quality attributes and relevance order of quality attributes. Identification of facial image working groups around the world. Opinion convergences between practical and technical user-experts, opinion divergences between practical and technical user-experts.

The group of requirements in a precedence order which best describe the quality for technical user-experts is:

- Head pose angle

- Width and length of head

Table 5.13: Relevance of Attributes According to Technical User Experts (TUE) and Practial User Experts (PUE)

Relevance	Attribute Order (TUE)	Attribute Order (PUE)
27	Expression	Head
26	No red eye	Brightness
25	Head	Size
24	Background	Contrast
23	Size	Antiquity
22	Antiquity	Expression
21	Vertical position of eyes	Horizontally centered face
20	No flash reflection	Width of head
19	Width of head	Background
18	Horizontally centered face	Head pose angle
17	Resolution	No flash reflection
16	Brightness	Resolution
15	Length of head	Vertical position
14	Head pose angle	No red eye
13	Contrast	Length of head
12	Focus	Focus
11	Lighting scene	Lighting scene
10	Dermis	Dermis
9	Eyes	Eyes
8	Facing	Facing
7	Percentage	Percentage
6	Exposure	Exposure
5	Mouth	Mouth
4	Color	Color
3	File	File
2	Number of faces	Number of faces
1	Distance between center of both eyes	Distance between center of both eyes

- Distribution of head

- Face features are recognizable

For practical user-experts group of requirements in a precedence order is:

- Brightness

- Contrast

- No red eye

- Eyes visibility

- Mouth closed

Other results obtained from the survey are the definition of the quality concept in a general sense, definition of facial image quality concept, relationships between security and facial image control, convergences and divergences of user-experts opinions with the conformance requirements of the standards mentioned previously, order of precedence of quality attributes and order of relevance of quality attributes. The identification of research groups working with face image and/or in biometrics around the world is another result of the survey.

Chapter 6

Determination of Reference Values for Image Quality Attributes

This thesis is based on the unalterable principle of *finding or developing algorithms for the determination of facial image quality without a reference image*. Quality is not absolute and to obtain a quality measure it is necessary to detect under which conditions a passport photo is considered as a good quality photo. The measurement of the photos quality conducts to:

- Calculation of attributes values of each element of the *good quality* data set

- Registration of all measured characteristics and statistical data description

- Obtention of an optimal value of each attribute

- Definition of *good quality ground truth for passport photos*

Ground truth data set a precedent of quality measuring of the attributes within specified accuracy and precision. The effectiveness of the ground truth should be tested in a reference values phase using a *bad quality* dataset.

6.1 Determination of Face Image Quality

The measurement methods for image attributes produce values as results towards the evaluated attribute. This means that there is no determination if the result is a valid and good value or not. Actually all metrics developed for calculating image quality like the works of [73], [75], [77], [74] need a reference image in order to work properly. The measurement of the differences permits to identify the best and the worst image. In a 2D image the image processing highly depends on the quality of an image. The image quality is always affected by external parameters from the environment e.g illumination [39]. It is difficult to detect a 2D face feature in various poses or expressions because some features vanish. Image quality can not be quantified by a single metric and quality measures must be calculated without a reference image. There are different methods to measure image attributes as shown in chapter two; the results just give the value of the evaluated attribute but nothing more, i.e. that there is no manner to know if the result can be considered as valid or not.

In chapter two the analysis of international standards [48], [4] related with facial image quality was explained. Requirements were identified through the implementation of the *Achto Cualli* method, the results obtained were three matrices: *1)Achto Cualli Matrix of Photograph Requirements, 2)Achto Cualli Matrix of Image Requirements, 3)Achto Cualli Matrix of Biometric Requirements.* Each matrix contains an attribute's list conformed by the conformance requirements sentences specified in the standards.

In the present chapter a method for measuring the magnitude of considered *"good quality"* face image attributes is developed. Characteristics and/or conditions using the known good quality samples and one or more related algorithms to measure their attributes as well as uncertainty and extrapolation ground truth model are specified. The algorithms to be explained in this chapter were implemented by Juan Guerrero [27], the design of the solution, methodologies, experiments, results and final metrics were produced by the author of this thesis.

6.2 Achto Pohua: A Method to Calibrate Facial Image Quality

Achto Pohua[1], this method proposes a hybrid model solution to determine the quality of digital passport photos. It was created after the identification of different processes concerned with the development and implementation of series of methods to identify, to process and to assess the image quality of facial images as biometric samples. The first method identified is to establish an inventory of existing image quality studies, quality assessment methods, metrics and an identification of characteristics associated to "good" quality passport photos.

An analysis for quality determinating characteristics of face images is essential to be performed in order to determine the parameters that will integrate the ground truth. Those parameters will permit to discover or to define the methods and/or metrics for integrating a consummate face image quality metric. The first step in developing more detailed qualitative models (such as mathematical models or software systems) to design the final solution of a problem is the creation of a conceptual model which helps to understand the problem and to identify the possible solution. Figure 6.1 represents the conceived conceptual model to determine a face image quality metric. This conceptual model is divided into three phases:

1. Analysis

2. Groundtruth sizing

3. Outcome

Each phase is a theoretical entity which must be developed through methods to obtain the results expected. The conceptualization of a ground truth assists to measure the magnitude of *"good quality"* facial image parameters.

The implementation of the conceptual model has given as result a method which is named *Achto Pohua*. It can be visualized in Figure 6.2 which represents the workflow of this method

---

[1]Achto means firstly, Pohua means to count in Nahuatl an ancient mexican language, the whole meaning is firstly counting

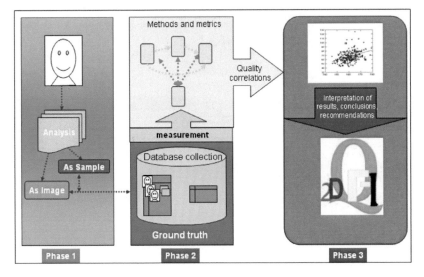

Figure 6.1: Conceptual Model to Find a Face Image Quality Metric

and the results expected after the development of each procedure. This method is compiled of ten procedures:

1. Samples enrollment according to conformance requirements

2. Sample database collecting

3. Sample database image analysis

4. Analysis of image attributes

5. Determining metrics for image quality attributes

6. Determining calibration values for image quality attributes

7. Analysis of biometric content

8. Determining quality metrics for biometric content

9. Determining calibration values for biometric content

10. Determining final quality metrics for digital passport photographs

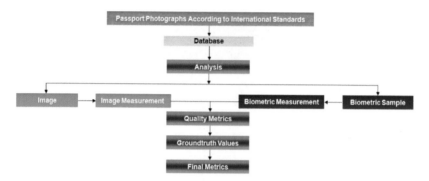

Figure 6.2: Achto Pohua Method to Obtain Quality Metrics for Digital Passport Photographs

6.3 Enrollment of Samples According to Conformance Requirements

The enrollment of samples in accordance with conformance requirements is achieved by supervising and controlling every detail of the scenario with the objective to take photographs under strict quality control from a portion of the population to study. For the purposes of this thesis and because of the nature and costs of the working material such as the rent of the photo studio, the payment of a professional in photography, the time and number of the individuals needed with special characteristics, the statistical method used is a sampling technique that implies the necessity to take a relatively small sample over a very short period of time named Design of Experiments (DoE) [3]. Using this technique the results obtained are usually instantaneous, permit to know the tendency of the whole population and allow to focus and control better the data processing stage. The population of this study were the employees of the Fraunhofer Institute for Computer Graphics Darmstadt whose number of employees is 372. The sample is the 6% of the population including men and women older than 18 years and covering different characteristics specified in Table 6.2. Figure 6.3 shows the scenario preparation scheme.

.

6.3.1 Scenario Preparation

The scene for the taking of photographs was prepared under the following conditions:

- Digital mirror reflex camera CANON EOS 20 D

- Lens objective Canon EFs 25-55mm

- Light electronic flash equipment CANON 580 EX

Table 6.1: *Achto Pohua* Procedures Specification

	Procedure	Ingoing data	Outgoing data
1	Sample enrollment	standards requirements specification, population of study identification and documentation, enrollment	sample data set with *good quality* controlled parameters
2	Database collecting and database analysis	sample data set	parameters documentation, design of experiments plan and testing plan
3	Analysis of image attributes	inventory of algorithms	inventory of metrics
4	Determining metrics for image quality attributes	sample data set, design of experiments plan, inventory of algorithms and metrics	attribute metrics implementation
5	Determining calibration values for image quality attributes	attribute metrics implementation, testing plan	testing results
6	Analysis of biometric content	inventory of algorithms	inventory of metrics
7	Determining calibration values for biometric content	sample data set, design of experiments plan, inventory of algorithms and metrics	attribute metrics implementation
8	Determining calibration values for biometric content	biometric content metrics implementation and testing plan	testing results
9	Determine final quality metrics for digital passport photographs	image attributes quality index, biometric content quality index, testing plan	final quality metric for digital passport photographs

- Lightning plant "Elinchrom" (1 x lightning head "Prolinca 500 s": 50 cycles per second, 240 v, with soft box 60 x 60cm, 2 x Spot "Prolinca 250": 100 Watts)

- Lightning plant "Hensel" (1 x lightning head "versus E 500" : 50-60 cycles per second, 230 v, with soft box 70 x 70 cm, 1 x Spot "versus E 250", 50-60 cycles per second, 230 V, max 300 Watts, on floor stand)

- Background: Cardboard smoothly, light-grey, approx. 250 g, width: 120 cm of digital values: ASA: 400/screen: 5,6/ time: 1/60 1/100/AWB/Autom.

- Lightning synchronous time

- Color mode: RGB

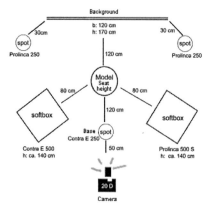

Figure 6.3: Scenario Preparation

6.3.2 Sample Capturing

A total of 24 persons with different characteristics described in Table 6.2 have been photographed. This set of digital facial images is named the *Cualli data set* and the original format of the images is PNG (Portable Network Graphics) format. PNG format is of principal value for images with large areas of exactly uniform color, it supports 16 million colors and is a lossless compression format. The *Cualli data set* is saved in a compressed format JPG (Joint Photograph Experts Group).

Normally a data set is analyzed as whole but in this case a segmentation is necessary. Each segment is considered as another population. Every conclusion, decision or result obtained will be representative for the segment not for the population. The statistical confidence must be focused on each segment, not on the population.

6.4 Importance of Data Set Classification by Skin Color

The skin color is one of the most conspicuous ways in which humans vary and has been widely used to define human ethnic groups [32]. The skin color has its own color distribution

Table 6.2: Characteristics of the People Photographed

Quantity	Characteristics
10	Female
14	Male
24	Ages between 18 - 64 years old
19	Caucasian
2	Asian
2	Amerind
1	African

that differs from that of most of non-face objects [63]. According to some authors who have been working with face images, the skin color affects the image quality primarily because it occupies a relatively large area [15] in facial images. The skin color can be used to determine the ethnic group of a person. The importance of identifying the ethnic group of a person is that every human ethnic group has particular characteristics that can be considered in the face recognition. The concept *ethnic group* is losing validity but it is still used by some scientists and since long time ago there is a discussion about the term. The genome scientists still do not have any agreement about the correct term to be used. "Today, scientists are faced with this situation in genomics, where existing biological models or paradigms of *racial* and *ethnic* categorizations cannot accommodate the uniqueness of the individual and universality of humankind that is evident in new knowledge emerging from human genome sequence variation research and molecular anthropological research. The paradigms of human identity based on *ethnic groups* as biological constructs are being questioned in light of the preponderance of data of human genome sequence variation and reflect the need for a new explanatory framework and vision of humankind with different fundamental assumption about biological groups that can accommodate new knowledge from a new generation of research. Discourse on the validity of *racial* categorization is certainly not new and will perhaps continue for generations to come" [7].

For practical reasons and because the objective of this thesis is not discuss the human genome or the human ethnic groups details, the concept *ethnic group* is used in this section for a better explanation of the main topic. The ethnic groups considered are according to Lewontin's classification mentioned in[18]: Caucasian, African, Mongoloid, S. Asian Aborigines, Amerinds, Oceanians, Australian Aborigines.

There are physical characteristics related to every human ethnic group and they are determined by genes; for example: body size, skin color and facial features such as form and size of eyelids, dimension and form of face, form and natural color of lips. Anthropometry is the biological science of human body measurement. Anthropometric data informs about the human factors that can help to design a wide variation of products to fit most people with the same characteristics.

In medicine, quantitative comparison of anthropometric data with patients' measurements before and after a plastic or reconstructive surgery furthers planning and assessment of plastic and reconstructive surgery. In forensic anthropology, conjectures about likely measurements derived from anthropometry, figure in the determination of individuals' appearance from their remains; and in the recovery of missing children, by aging their anthropometry and appearance taken from photographs [14].

"Anthropometric evaluation begins with the identification of particular locations on a subject, named *landmark* points, defined in terms of visible or palpable features (skin or bone) on the subject. Two of the landmarks determine a canonical horizontal orientation for the head. The horizontal plane is determined by the two lines (on either side of the head) connecting the landmark *t* to the landmark *or* (for orbitale), the lowest point of the eye socket on the skull. In measurement, anthropometrists actually align the head to this horizontal what is known as Frankfurt horizontal (FH) position. A vertical mid-line axis is defined by the landmarks *n* (for *nasion*), a skull feature roughly between the eyebrows; *sn* (for *subnasale*) the center point where the nose meets the upper lip; and *gn* (for *gnathion*), the lowest point of the chin. Farka's inventory includes the five types of facial measurements:

- the *shortest distance* between two landmarks. An example is *en-ex*, the distance between landmarks at the corners of the eye.

- the *axial distance* between two landmarks - the distance measured along one of the axes of the canonical coordinate system, with the head in FH position. An example is *v-tr*, the vertical distance (height difference) between the top of the head (*v* for *vertex*) and hairline (*tr* for *trichion*).

- the *tangential distance* between two landmarks -the distance measured along a prescribed path on the surface distance from the corner of the mouth (*ch* for *cheilion*) to the tragus.

- the *angle of inclination* between two landmarks with respect to one of the canonical axes. An example is the inclination of the ear axis with respect to the vertical.

- the *angle between locations*, such as the mentocervical angle (the angle at the chin)

Figure 6.5 shows the face landmarks and an example of facial measures mentioned above. A total of 132 measurements on the face and head are described by Farkas; some measurements are *paired*, when there is a corresponding measurement on the left and right side of the face. The measurement process works in the last years has investigated 3D range scanners as an alternative to manual measurement. Subjects have been grouped on the basis of gender, ethnic group, age or the presence of a physical syndrome. Means and variances for the measurements within a group provide a series of measurements which capture virtually all of the variation that can occur in the group. Many facial proportions have been found to show statistically significant differences across population groups" [14]. Figure 6.6 shows the difference of landmarks and anthropometric measurements in individuals from different ethnic groups.

The color of human hair and skin is determined by the presence of pigments named melanins; variation in cutaneous melanin pigmentation in humans has been attributed to many factors, with most authorities agreeing that the observed variations reflect biological adaptations to some aspect of the environment. Skin color is adaptive and it is related to the regulation of

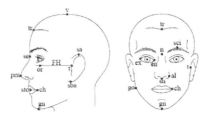

Figure 6.4: Anthropometric Landmarks on the Face [14]

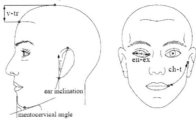

Figure 6.5: Example Anthropometric Measurements[14]

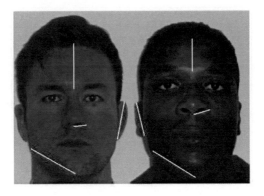

Figure 6.6: Anthropometric Differences between Persons from Different Ethnic Groups. [53]

ultraviolet (UV) radiation levels. Vitamin D_3 is essential for normal growth, calcium absorption and skeletal development. Deficiency of the vitamin can cause death, immobilization, or pelvic deformities which prevent normal childbirth. Apart from its beneficial role in vitamin D synthesis, the effects of UVB radiation on the skin are universally harmful. Suppression of sweating and subsequent disruption of thermo regulation due to sunburn induced damage to sweat glands are the most serious immediate effects of excessive UVB exposure. In the skin, melanin acts as an optical and chemical photo protective filter, which is the quantity of UV radiation required to produce a barely perceptible reddening of lightly-pigmented skin. Epidermal melanin has different forms at different sites with radiation, most of studies of the effects of UV radiation on human skin have utilized as a standard the minimum-erythemal dose (UVMED) which is the quantity of UV radiation required to produce a barely percepti- ble reddening of lightly-pigmented skin. Hypotheses concerning the distribution of the skin color of indigenous peoples relative to UV levels [32] appear in the last years. Jablonski et. al. in 2000 published a map of predicted skincolor for modern terrestrial environments, a re- gression was computed between annual average UVMED and the observed skin reflectance. The observed reflectances for indigenous populations were based on all available data for a particular area or group.

Three zones representing different potentials for UV-induced vitamin D_3 synthesis in light- skinned humans were identified. Figure 6.7 represents the map with predicted skin color distribution[32]. The colors reflect the degree of ultraviolet radiation at different latitudes. Background patterns illustrate three zones of human skin tone. Zone 1 contains tropical peo- ples with the darkest skin color, the skin of people native to Zone 2 possesses the most po- tential for growing lighter or darker seasonally, Zone 3 natives have paler skin to make up for lower levels of sunlight.

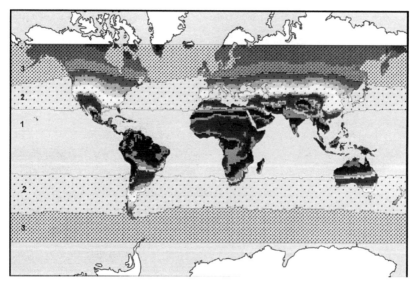

Figure 6.7: Skin Color Distribution According to Reflection Degree of Ultraviolet Radiation Published in year 2000

Figure 6.8: Biasutti's Map of the Distribution of Skin Color Published in 1954[56]

Around 1940, Renato Biasutti published a book titled "Le Razze e i popoli della terra" in which map "Distribuzione della Varia Intensita del Colore della Pelle" was published and it has been considered as the most straightforward way of showing how the skin color varies regionally, Biasutti's map is presented in Figure 6.8.

The purpose of this thesis is to produce results that can be projected for similar cases using the know-how presented here. Following this principle the most representative group of facial images classified by skin color will be used. A skin color likelihood model can be derived from skin color samples [63]. The *Cualli data set* was segmented into five subsets:

- D1. All photos presented in Figure 6.9

- D2. All photos except from persons with African characteristics presented in Figure 6.10

- D3. All photos from persons who have Caucasian skin color presented in Figure 6.11

- D4. All D3 photos organized by gender presented in Figure 6.12

- D5. All D3 photos from eyeglass wearers. This set is subcategorized into two sub-sets: the same person with and without eyeglasses presented in Figure 6.13

The set with the biggest number and variety of common characteristics of elements to study is D3. Skin color is mostly used as approximate localization and segmentation of faces in the camera image. In order to reduce the search area for other more precise and computationally expensive facial feature detection methods [46]. A skin color set segmentation was conducted which is one of the most important criteria to obtain more representative statistics for the German or European population.

6.5   Design of Experiments

The *Cualli dataset* analysis is made considering different determinant factors such as file type (compressed or uncompressed), data set (D1, D2, D3, D4 and D5), color space and some of

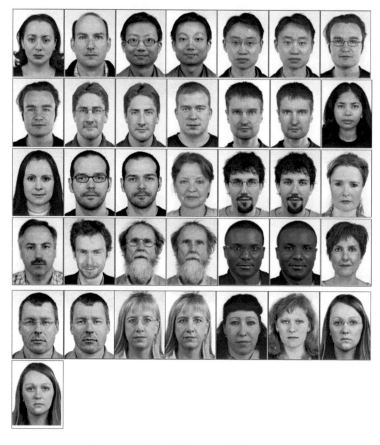

Figure 6.9: D1 Cualli Dataset, All Photographs

the image quality attributes defined by Keelan [37] like noise, contrast and brightness. To visualize, structure and classify the factors to consider in the database analysis, a mind map can be found in Figure 6.15. For compressed files the format JPG (of the Joint Photographic Experts Group) is considered. All photo's files are compressed into this file type; originally the files are in an uncompressed format PNG (PorLtable Network Graphics). It supports true color (16 million colors) and this format is recommended for photograph experts because it is a lossless format and is the best suited for pictures. There are seventeen factors to be analyzed; a combination of all factors grouped by dataset gives as result 6188 possible number of experiments to be developed according to formula 6.1

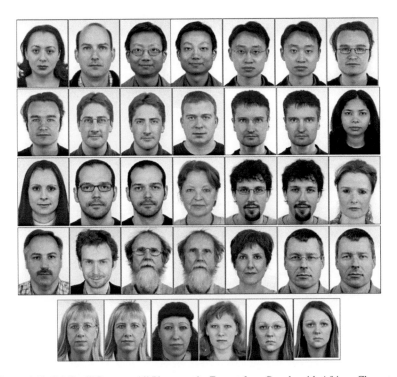

Figure 6.10: D2 Cualli Dataset, All Photographs Except from People with African Characteristics

$$C_{m,n} = \frac{m!}{n! * (m - n)!}$$
$$C_{17,5} = \frac{17!}{5! * (17 - 5)!};$$
$$C_{17,5} = 6188$$

(6.1)

In scientific research the experimentation phase is important to discover interesting aspects of a process or system under test. To set up experiments there are often used adhoc approaches or one factor at a time methods [30] with a large number of experiments. Frequently more experiments are run than necessary or a sub-optimal selection of tests is run without obtaining the desired results. Design of Experiments (DoE) is a systematic approach to find out most relevant aspects about a system or process [3].

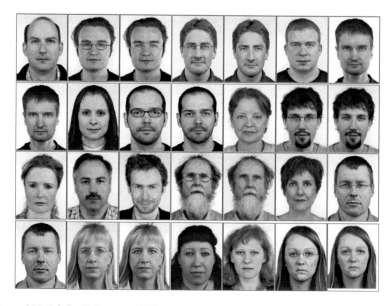

Figure 6.11: D3 Cualli Dataset, All Photographs from People with Caucasian Characteristics

Series of structured tests are designed in which planned changes are made to the input variables of a process or system. The effects of these changes on a pre-defined output are then
assessed. Exhaustive experimentation consumes time and resources. That consumption can
be avoided using DoE; DoE is a two-step process that begins with a structured approach to
set up experiments and culminates with a statistical analysis. DoE is important as a formal
way of maximizing information gained while minimizing resources required. This systematic
approach can be used to find answers in situations where the different factors involved interact
with each other contributing in the variation of the last results. In general, these situations are
given label as particular types of study. Formulation of key questions gives parameter design
and robustness study, every key question of DoE is used to find the answer identifying the
influence level of each factor to be analyzed. For each input variable, a number of levels is
defined to represent the range for which the effect of that variable is desired to be known. An
experimental plan is produced which tells the experimenter where to set each test parameter
for each run of the test. The principle of DoE involves designing a set of ten to twenty experiments; for this work a set of twelve experiments was selected in which the relevant factors
such as file type, color space, data set and the algorithms for contrast, brightness and noise
are varied systematically. Figure 6.14 shows a mind map of the Design of Experiments; there
are twelve experiments from which six are for JPG (compressed) files and six are for PNG
(uncompressed) files. Those experiments should be made for each data set (D1, D2, D3, D4,

Figure 6.12: D4 Cualli Dataset, the Same as D3 Grouped by Gender

D5). Figure 6.15 shows the factors to be evaluated in these experiments.

6.5.1 Techniques

The analysis and experimentation is developed in different phases.

- Application of contrast, brightness and noise algorithms to each file type PNG and JPG files with the following color spaces:

  - CIE XYZitu D65
  - Hue saturation value
  - CIE Lab D65
  - Hue saturation brightness
  - Hue saturation lightness
  - Normalized RGB

- Obtain the descriptive statistics, classify data sets and decide the method to evaluate each data set

Figure 6.13: D5 Cualli Dataset, the Same as D3 Grouped by Eyeglasses Wearers

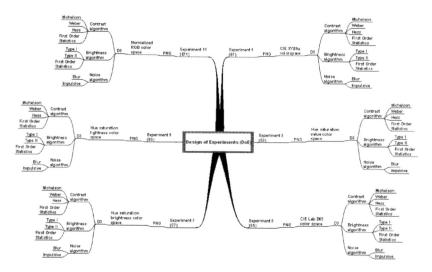

Figure 6.14: Mindmap: Design of Experiments to Calibrate a Face Image

Table 6.3: A Segment of Design of Experiments for Analyzing of the Data Set

ID	File type	Color space	Data set	Algorithm	Expected results
E1	PNG	CIE XYZ-itu	D1, D2, D3, D4, D5	Contrast: Michelson, Weber, Hess, First Order Statistics. Brightness: Type I, Type II, First Order Statistics. Noise: Blur, Impulsive	Contrast, brightness, noise indexes for D1, D2, D3, D4, D5 in uncompressed files with CIE XYZitu color space
E2	JPG	CIE XYZ-itu	D1, D2, D3, D4, D5	Contrast: Michelson, Weber, Hess, First Order Statistics. Brightness: Type I, Type II, First Order Statistics. Noise: Blur, Impulsive	Contrast, brightness, noise indexes for D1, D2, D3, D4, D5 in compressed files with CIE XYZitu color space
E3	PNG	Hue saturation value	D3	Contrast: Michelson, Weber, Hess, First Order Statistics. Brightness: Type I, Type II, First Order Statistics. Noise: Blur, Impulsive	Contrast, brightness, noise indexes for D3 in uncompressed files with hue saturation value color space

- Test whether readily identified factors affect the results in a significant manner, as determined in the previous step

- Use analysis of results, classifying data sets in subsets

- Determine which is the best algorithm for each attribute with this file type and for each color space based on variation of the fit parameters across subsets and sequential tests

- Obtain hypotheses and conclusions

- Test the hypotheses with a different dataset

- Obtain results and conclusions

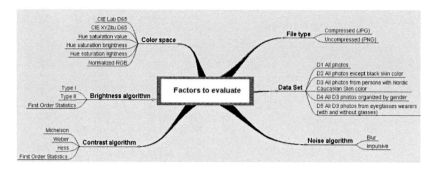

Figure 6.15: Evaluating Factors to Analyze the Sample Database

6.5.2   Skin Color Identification

Knowing the skin color is essential to interpret the results of the algorithms to be applied, the algorithm used to detect the skin color is the *Elliptic Boundary Model (EBM)*. It uses a unimodal Gaussian algorithm with a fixed probability threshold for skin detection, giving the same result as using an elliptical boundary around the mean value of the distribution [38]. With the elliptical boundary model [38] it is possible to detect skin and not skin color regions through histograms. To test this theory experiments were performed with the different datasets. Figure 6.16 shows the original skin color histogram (left side). The skin color is concentrated in the blue-red part. The black background has a value of zero, which implies that there is no skin color contribution from these colors. In Figure 6.16 the difference between a good skin color detection can be easily appreciated on the right side. Figure 6.16 shows a bad skin color detection, there is a black ellipse that represents no skin color, the little ellipse inside represents the skin color.

This analysis verifies that, with the actual characteristics of the *Cualli dataset*, it is possible to generate good skin color histograms identification. If there was the same quantity of input data for all ethnic groups the ellipses could be recomputed as long as necessary to find the best one that encloses the skin color portion in the color space to be applied. The clear identification of the skin color is possible through the computation of histograms for all colorspaces and selecting those three spaces that allow to identify the three different ethnic groups (skin colors). After the skin color identification the ROI is extracted, and the algorithms of contrast, brightness, impulsive noise and blur are computed.

6.5.3   Results of Experiments

The results of the first experiment $E1$ were applied in CIE XYZitu. The color space establishes quantification of quality changes arising from preferential attributes is substantially more complex, because the objective metrics are composed of terms that depend on the preference and because preference varies with each subset and skin color. During the skin color analysis and segmentation the target population was defined from people with *Caucasian*

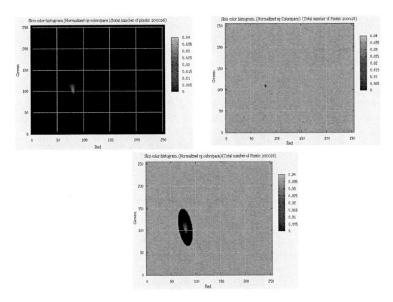

Figure 6.16: Skin Color Histogram

characteristics. The rest of experiments was applied to this data set *D3* and from now on in this thesis the data set to study is referred to as *Cualli dataset*. The research questions are:

- Which data set is the most representative sampling frame from the whole population?

- Which data set shows minimum skin color variation?

- Which data set produces the smallest threshold of results from most of algorithms?

The results of the first group of experiments *E1*, show the significant affection which the skin color has on all brightness indexes. This affection expresses itself in the size of the brightness type I interval. While for $D1$ the interval is $I_I \in [0.3094501492, 0.6770204295]$, the brightness type I interval of $D2$ is $I_{II} \in [0.5981283353, 0.6770204295]$ which represents a shorter difference between the two limits in $D2$. It means that an efficient brightness metric can only be defined, if the photos are sorted according to the skin color. The most suggested brightness metric is on the interval $I \in [0, 1]$.

The allocation according to the different skin colors is compacted and thus a very favorable distribution of the brightness numbers of the optimal passport photos is required. An investigation of the different contrast indices shows that the skin color contrast has fewer affection than the brightness. This is comprehensible if one considers that the contrast defines the relationship between the absolute values of the bright and dark intensities within a certain range, while only the absolute values of the intensity are used in the region to brightness computation.

The absolute value of the intensity is naturally independent of skin color; however the relationship of the absolute value is not in a certain region. In other words, the contrast is through light dark transitions and in the state of edges and outlines. During the brightness measurement excluding the intensity value of the regarded pixel enters measured value, while during the contrast always measures not only the environment of the regarded pixel but also the light and dark sample measured value. These light and dark samples arise mostly at edges and outlines and the occurrence of these edges and face outlines primarily by the face physiognomy and are not absolute determined by the skin color. The dataset $D3$ contains facial images just from people with Caucasian characteristics, other facial images from other persons are not considered. A comparison brightness of the $D2$ dataset mean $I_{II} \in [0.5981283353, 0.6770204295]$ with the brightness index of $D3$ dataset $I_{III} \in [0.5981283353, 0.6770204295]$ shows that both indexes intervals are identical. In fact it infers that the range of values of facial images from Asian and Amerindo people are not different from Caucasian people.

Tests for $D4$ show that for all brightness means, the intervals of the women indexes are always a subinterval of the men brightness indexes. The brightness mean of men is smaller than of women. It is reasonable that men beard structure is a part of the bright face skin which is covered and thus the face appears darker so it leads to a smaller mean. On the other hand the face can be lighted by whiskers which are brighter than the skin color of the regarded person, which leads to more brightness mean than with women. The difference between women and men mean is caused by the beard of some men. It can be inferred that the hair over the face region affects to find a brightness threshold for people with the same skin color. For $D5$ results show that the brightness and contrast mean of all photos from persons with eyeglasses, the range appears darker than the same range from persons without eyeglass. Since the brightness number is determined by summing the absolute intensity values of the pixels, the occurrence of regions with lower intensity values (the region, which is covered by the eyeglasses) is expected to decrease the brightness number of the entire face. The light dark conditions are received for computing the contrast number. After this process the contrast for a determined area for a subsection, which is covered by the eyeglasses is received. It can be expected that due to the smaller prevailing intensity compared with the contrast value the determined contrast would be varied for the same area without eyeglasses. Since the *Cualli dataset* is created under strict conditions, the ranges for blur and impulsive noise are too small tending to be zero. The twelve experiments were made for $D3$ dataset in the two file formats: JPG and PNG in the six colorspaces mentioned in the previous sections. inferred in previous subjective analysis that $D3$ can be the most significant data set, it was necessary to do a test to prove that hypothesis. The results obtained for *Cualli dataset* would yield some tendencies that can be projected for a bigger population composed by people with the same characteristics like most of European citizens.

As conclusions of the experiments, can be determined that:

- Preliminary results show that the rest of experiments can be significant just for people with Caucasian characteristics.

- D1 data set (all files) is not statistically representative for all ethnic groups and skin colors.

- D3 data set (all photos from people with Caucasian characteristics) is statistically representative for Caucasian skin color.

- The European beard type is different from the Asians, and beard affects the brightness index.

- An identification of skin color threshold for the Asian and Amerind in a deeper level will establish new indexes for these skin colors.

- If the face with eyeglasses is not positioned in the right position occurs reflection in the eyeglasses.

- In the evaluated data set eyeglasses, which are reflecting light make unrecognizable the iris and pupils, this set of photographs not cover the ICAO specifications,therefore digital face images with such eyeglasses are not part of the regarded data record.

- If passport photographs from persons who have a reflecting side or reflecting glasses with or without eyeglass frameworks produced an increased contrast and brightness index.

- If the indexes obtained would be applied in a quality metric, it is reliable just for face images from people with Caucasian characteristics.

6.6   Image Quality Attributes

The results of the inferences derivated from the best algorithm for each attribute according to the file type and color space were proved through tests with different facial images. Every new sample has the same characteristics as the other: It must be from women or men with Caucasian characteristics.

The identification of the best algorithm to measure every attribute is based on the result how well they can discriminate a "perfect" facial image like one of the *Cualli dataset* from a "bad" facial image. Figure 6.17 shows the criteria to select an algorithm. It is based on a comparison between the range values of the ground truth G from every algorithm of the attribute a obtained from *Cualli dataset D3* in every colorspace and the values calculated for a certain set of facial images considered as "bad quality". This last set is compound of facial images that were altered in the contrast and brightness properties and for some others a noise function was applied.

Following this criteria and assuming that

In the next list the conditions to accept an algorithm as valid are shown. The definitions of variables are located in Table 6.4:

1. $V_x(a_{C1}) \notin (G_{min}(a_{C1}), G_{max}(a_{C1}))$ or

2. $V_x(a_{C2}) \notin (G_{min}(a_{C2}), G_{max}(a_{C2}))$ or

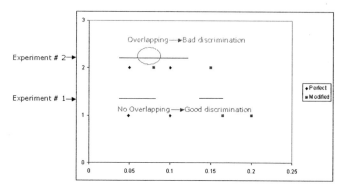

Figure 6.17: Criteria to Select an Algorithm

3. $V_x(a_{C3}) \not\equiv (G_{min}(a_{C3}), G_{max}(a_{C3}))$ or

4. $V_x(a_{C4}) \not\equiv (G_{min}(a_{C4}), G_{max}(a_{C4}))$ and

5. $V_x(a_{B1}) \not\equiv (G_{min}(a_{B1}), G_{max}(a_{B1}))$ or

6. $V_x(a_{B2}) \not\equiv (G_{min}(a_{B2}), G_{max}(a_{B2}))$ and

7. $V_x(a_{N1}) \not\equiv (G_{min}(a_{N1}), G_{max}(a_{N1}))$ or

8. $V_x(a_{N2}) \not\equiv (G_{min}(a_{N2}), G_{max}(a_{N2}))$

The algorithms were compared through the root mean square (RMS) as statistical measure of
the magnitude of varying quantity; it can be calculated for a series of discrete values. The
RMS must be normalized to avoid large differences. Naturally this score tends particularly to
be sensitive to large differences and to any data field smoothing or filtering in the analysis and
forecast model. Another evaluation was made using *Radar Plot or Spiderweb Plot*. A radar
plot permits to look at several different factors all related to one item. They have multiple
axes along which data can be plotted. For the algorithms' evaluation the representation of the
algorithms' data was done as follows: on one axis the colorspaces are plotted, another axis
shows the attribute to evaluate, the last axis shows the scale of values. The plots produced
are hexagons, there are six colorspaces to be evaluated and for every colorspace there are four
attributes to evaluate with different algorithms. One can compare the results of all attributes
for a certain colorspace at the same time in one radar plot; for example Figure 6.18 shows
the first radar chart produced. The diagram shows different regular hexagons and the biggest
is an irregular one. The data source of the diagram are the values that conform the interval
calculated for the *Cualli dataset* for every algorithm and for every type of file. The biggest
hexagons are the maximal value calculated for contrast with the first order statistics formula
and for brightness with the formula for brightness type II. Both values determine a too broad
interval data and could not be a good reference as ground truth. With the radar plot one can see

Table 6.4: List of Algorithms to be Evaluated

Variable	Meaning
a_{C1}	Michelson Contrast
a_{C2}	Weber Contrast
a_{C3}	Hess Contrast
a_{C4}	First Order Statistics Contrast
a_{B1}	Brightness Type I
a_{B2}	Brightness Type II
a_{N1}	Impulsive Noise
a_{N2}	Blur Noise
G	represents the reference values value
V_x	represents the calculated value of an algorithm from a x facial image

that every attribute has a different scale of values. The differences between algorithms cannot be clearly appreciated, but one can see the data distribution. Then in this first evaluation the algorithms previously mentioned were discarded.

The second evaluation was done comparing the values of *Cualli dataset* with a set of facial images that is integrated for facial images with similar characteristics like number of people, skin color and size. The experiments were conducted evaluating the conditions to accept an algorithm previously mentioned. Not all conditions were covered, and the algorithms which accomplished more conditions were selected as good algorithms. As conclusion of this analysis the following algorithms gave the best results. The formulas used are included in this section, nevertheless they were detailed in chapter four of this work referred to image quality.

- Contrast, Michelson[52]

$$C_M = \frac{I_{max} - I_{min}}{I_{max} + I_{min}}; \quad \text{with: } C_M \in [0, 1] \tag{6.2}$$

where I_{max} and I_{min} are the maximum and minimum intensity value, valid ranges are from $[0, 1]$

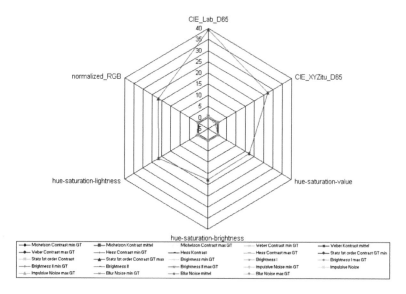

Figure 6.18: Radar Plot with All Calculated Attributes for Uncompressed Files with Corresponding Ground Truth

- Brightness, Type I [10]

$$\overline{H} = \frac{\sum\limits_{i=1}^{w*h} P(i)}{w * h * I_{max}}, \text{ with: } \qquad \begin{aligned} &P(i) : \text{Gray value} \\ &I_{max} : \text{max. Intensity value} \\ &w : \text{Image width} \\ &h : \text{Image height} \end{aligned} \qquad (6.3)$$

The valid values vary between 0 and 1, whereas 0 means the absolute darkness and 1 is the maximum brightness.

- Blur Noise, Blurring [43]

$$BlurMeasure = TotBM/NbEdges \text{ and } TotBM = \sum_{i=0}^{n}(P_i' - P_i) \qquad (6.4)$$

in which $TotBM$ is the total blur measurement composed by the summatory of edges width. The edge width is $(P_i' - P_i)$, i is the edge located, P defines the start position, while the local minimum P' corresponds to the end position.

- Impulsive Noise, based on the adaptive median filter of [40]

$$R_{\text{noise}} = \frac{\sum\limits_{x,y} \delta_{\widehat{P}(x,y),M(x,y)}}{w * h} [27] \qquad (6.5)$$

in which $\delta_{i,j}$ is the Delta value and is correlated through the discrete version of Delta named Kronecker-Delta and is defined as:

$$\delta_{\widehat{P}(x,y),M(x,y)} = \begin{cases} 1 & \text{if } \widehat{P}(x,y) = M(x,y) \\ 0 & \text{if } \widehat{P}(x,y) \neq M(x,y) \end{cases}$$

6.7   Ground Truth of Image Attributes

The central problem now is to quantify the optimal quality value of all attributes or parameters considering the data volume and characteristics variation and the intervals of each attribute. The phenomenon obtained is a stochastic model that varies depending on the resulting values of every attribute. This stochastic model uses the attributes values that are consistent with the whole distribution having as base the $\overline{x}$, maximal max_a and minimal min_a value of each attribute of the set; together they give an approximation of the exact evaluation. In artificial intelligence this concept is used to design stochastic simulations [58]. The concept stochastic is almost always associated with time series. It is most common in engineering. But stochastic refers to a process involving a randomly determined sequence of observations each of which is considered as a sample of one element from a probability distribution [9]. In this model there are random locations of points in an euclidean space composite for the set of attributes that determine if a facial image as the element x located in a data set is qualified as "good" or "bad" image depending on its attributes values.

A new formula presented in 6.6 that determines an optimal value for attributes is created as solution for this problem. This formula calculates T, it means *Teotl* [2]. T determines the optimal value obtained for an attribute and it varies according to the values of the *Cualli data set*.

$$T_a = \frac{\overline{x}_a - min_a}{max_a - min_a} \qquad (6.6)$$

where T_a is the optimal value for a attribute as contrast or brightness, $\overline{x}$ is the arithmetic mean, min_a is the minimal value of the range and max_a is the maximal value of the range. The indicator T is based on the values of $\overline{x}$ and the minimal and maximal value of the value interval from every attribute, T indicates the tendency of the attributes values, it is a special characteristic of T. One can expect that the values of an attribute of a facial image that can be considered as good must be between the value of T and the value of the arithmetic mean of *Cualli dataset*. This permits to know as how "good" or how "bad" the calculated value should be considered. The *Teotl* formula is tested using the *Cualli dataset* and using another data

---

[2]Teotl in Nahuatl an ancient Mexican language, means energy or light

set integrated for facial images obtained from [2], and some others from a private face image database. The test results of Formula 6.6 are organized according to type of file, attribute and colorspace.

6.7.1   Reference Values of Contrast

Table 6.5 and Figure 6.19 represent the calibrating values for the contrast. Normalized RGB colorspace presents the broadest interval and it can not be a good colorspace to evaluate the contrast; in CIE Lab D65, Hue saturation brightness, Hue saturation value and Hue saturation lightness colorspaces the value of T tends to be tighter than $\bar{x}$. It can be inferred as rule that:

- In the interval designated to measure the contrast, the value of an evaluated facial image must be between $\bar{x}$ and T where $T > \bar{x}$.

Table 6.5: Reference Values for Contrast Ordered by Colorspace

| | Contrast | | | |
| | Compressed Files | | Uncompressed Files | |
Colorspace	$\bar{x}$	T_c	$\bar{x}$	T_c
CIE Lab D65	0.033924	0.260014	0.036743	0.398913
CIE XYZitu D65	0.072880	0.442783	0.069934	0.376689
Hue saturation brightness	0.069005	0.238065	0.075131	0.256005
Hue saturation lightness	0.068032	0.240584	0.076406	0.270182
Hue saturation value	0.057673	0.238786	0.058672	0.239368
Normalized RGB	0.068581	0.763690	0.076690	0.272959

6.7.2   Reference Values of Brightness

Table 6.6 and Figure 6.20 represent the calibrating values for brightness. Cie XYZitu D65 colorspace presents the broadest interval between $\bar{x}$ and T_b; and it can not be a good colorspace to evaluate the brightness; in the rest of colorspaces the value of T_b tends to be shorter than $\bar{x}$. It can be inferred as rule that:

- In the interval designated to measure the brightness, the value of an evaluated facial image must be between $\bar{x}$ and T where $T \leq \bar{x}$

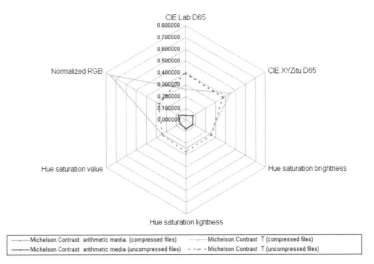

Figure 6.19: Contrast Reference Values

Table 6.6: Reference Values of Brightness Ordered by Colorspace

	Brightness			
	Compressed Files		Uncompressed Files	
Colorspace	$\bar{x}$	T_b	$\bar{x}$	T_b
CIE Lab D65	0.791974	0.724322	0.758546	0.900489
CIE XYZitu D65	0.590457	0.461411	0.574878	0.362486
Hue saturation brightness	0.587521	0.626862	0.564800	0.804947
Hue saturation lightness	0.601226	0.622542	0.602040	0.609340
Hue saturation value	0.719776	0.628783	0.721241	0.613412
Normalized RGB	0.588052	0.618014	0.586918	0.603930

6.7.3 Reference Values of Impulsive Noise

The impulsive noise has been evaluated in a different way. The presence of noise in a facial image is detected, there is a maximum value permitted for impulsive noise. T is the max-

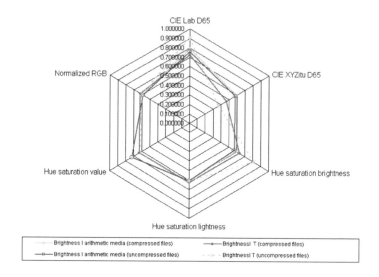

Figure 6.20: Brightness Reference Values

imum value calculated in the *Cualli dataset*; variable. Table 6.7 and Figure 6.21 represent the calibrating values for impulsive noise. The value of impulsive noise tends to be zero. In Cie XYZitu D65 colorspace presents the broadest interval between $\bar{x}$ and T for uncompressed files. The minimum value of impulsive noise is zero and when the evaluation of impulsive noise for a certain facial image is done the first constraint to be applied must be the control of impulsive noise value and this must be approximately or equal to zero or less than T. The inferred rule is:

- In the interval designated to measure the impulsive noise in a determined facial image, the value must be between $\bar{x}$ and T; where $\bar{x} \leq 0$

6.7.4 Reference Values of Blur Noise

The evaluation of blur noise is similar as for impulsive noise: the presence of noise in a facial image is detected, and a maximum value is permitted for blur noise. T is the maximum value calculated in the *Cualli dataset* variable. Table 6.8 and Figure 6.22 represent the calibrating values for blur noise. The value of blur noise tends to be zero, for blur noise there is no general rule related to colorspaces. The values of impulsive noise do not have a relationship with colorspace or file type. To evaluate this noise, colorspace must be defined previously to

Table 6.7: Reference Values of Impulsive Noise Ordered by Colorspace

| | Impulsive Noise | | | |
| | Compressed Files | | Uncompressed Files | |
Colorspace	$\overline{x}$	T_{in}	$\overline{x}$	T_{in}
CIE Lab D65	0.000154	0.002853	0.000244	0.006654
CIE XYZitu D65	0.000014	0.000087	0.000034	0.065557
Hue saturation brightness	0.000010	0.000050	0.000035	0.000679
Hue saturation lightness	0.000009	0.000050	0.000037	0.000731
Hue saturation value	0.000005	0.000050	0.000034	0.000697
Normalized RGB	0.000010	0.000052	0.000037	0.000679

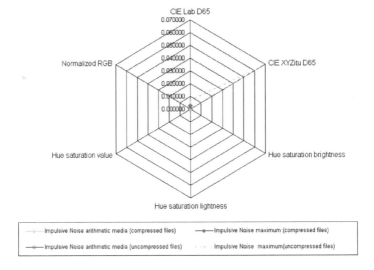

Figure 6.21: Impulsive Noise Reference Values

use the ground truth. For a certain facial image the second constraint to be applied must be to define the colorspace to be used. The inferred rule is:

- In the interval designated to measure the blur noise (blurring) of a certain facial image, the value must be between $\overline{x}$ and T_{bn}; where $\overline{x} \le T_{bn} \ge 0$

Table 6.8: Reference Values of Blurring Ordered by Colorspace

	Blur Noise			
	Compressed Files		Uncompressed Files	
Colorspace	$\overline{x}$	T_{bn}	$\overline{x}$	$T_b n$
CIE Lab D65	0.000109	0.000620	0.000150	0.001420
CIE XYZitu D65	0.000096	0.000715	0.000091	0.000082
Hue saturation brightness	0.000077	0.000654	0.001421	0.000286
Hue saturation lightness	0.000077	0.000652	0.000051	0.000294
Hue saturation value	0.000081	0.000740	0.000056	0.000386
Normalized RGB	0.000514	0.000046	0.000062	0.000308

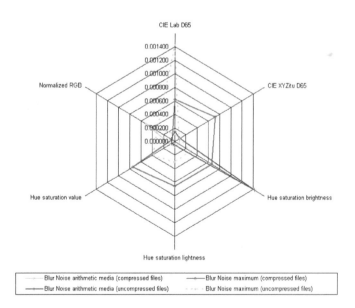

Figure 6.22: Blur Noise Reference Values

6.8   Image Attributes Quality Index Constraints

The image attributes quality index must express a value that indicates how "good" or how "bad" are the image attributes of an evaluated facial image. The determination of "good" and "bad" is given by the congruent relation of the variables involved, having as reference values of image attributes the information presented in Table 6.9

Table 6.9: Image Attributes Quality Constraints

Attribute	Calculated Parameters	Condition
Contrast	$\overline{x}_c, T_c$	$T_c > \overline{x}_c$
Brightness	$\overline{x}_b, T_b$	$T_b \leq \overline{x}_b$
Impulsive Noise	$\overline{x}_{in}, T_{in}$	$\overline{x}_{in} \leq T_{in}$
Blur Noise	$\overline{x}_{bn}, T_{bn}$	$\overline{x}_{bn} \leq T_{bn}$

Parameter $\overline{x}$ represents the arithmetic mean of a certain attribute in a certain colorspace, T determines the optimal value obtained for an attribute and its calculation varies according to the related attribute. Both parameters were calculated for the *Cualli data set* for different types of files. The interval values obtained for every attribute determine the acceptance threshold of "good" quality.

The ground truths defined above are valid under the following circumstances:

- The facial images used to define the ground truth are from people with caucasian characteristics

- The values presented correspond to compressed files (JPG) and uncompressed files (PNG)

- The reference values here defined are valid for facial images whose size is 413x531 pixels.

- The reference values presented here can be projected to a bigger dataset with the same controlled characteristics as the *Cualli dataset*.

6.9   Summary

A method named *Achto Pohua* was developed to solve the problem of finding a quality metric for facial images. This method was created after the identification of different processes concerned with the development of series of methods to identify, process and assess the image quality of biometric samples in this case facial images. The first method identified is to establish an inventory of existing image quality studies, quality assessment methods, metrics and an identification of characteristics associated to "good" quality passport photos. Figure 6.1

represents the conceived conceptual model to determine a face image quality metric. A selected population was photographed, the statistical method used is a sampling technique that implies to take a relatively small sample over a very short period of time named DoE (Design of Experiments) [3]. Using this technique the results obtained are usually instantaneous, permit to know the tendency of the whole population, and allows to take more care and control in the data processing stage. This set of digital facial images is named the *Cualli data set* and the original format of the images is PNG (Portable Network Graphics) format. PNG format is of principal value for images with large areas of exactly uniform color. It supports 16 million colors and is a lossless compression format. The *Cualli data set* is saved in a compressed format JPG (Joint Photograph Experts Group). The *Cualli data set* was segmented into five subsets:

- D1. All photos presented in Figure 6.9

- D2. All photos except from persons with African characteristics presented in Figure 6.10

- D3. All photos from persons who have Caucasian skin colorpresented in Figure 6.11

- D4. All D3 photos organized by genderpresented in Figure 6.12

- D5. All D3 photos from eyeglass wearers, this set is subcategorized in two sub-sets: the same person with and without eyeglasses presented in Figure 6.13

The set with most number and variety of common characteristics of elements to study is D3. Skin color is mostly used as approximate localization and segmentation of faces in the camera image. In order to reduce the search area for other more precise and computationally expensive facial feature detection methods [46] a skin color set segmentation was created which is one of the most important criteria to obtain more representative statistics for the German or European population.

Chapter 7

Determination of Reference Values for Biometric Quality Attributes

The photograph content related to characteristics of head region and face is interpreted as biometric content. The attributes of the biometric content identified in the analysis of the international standards ICAO/MRTD [48], and ISO 19794-5 [4] are: Head pose angle, width of head, length of head, number of faces, horizontally centered face, vertical position of the face, resolution of the head and eyes center. This chapter describes the biometric analysis of the *Cualli dataset* (set of photographs taken under controlled conditions with the best quality), with the purpose to develop methods to obtain the parameters that can be measured to define a quality index for the biometric content of a facial image. Series of algorithms were implemented to measure the quality of passport photographs as biometric sample. Some algorithms to be presented in this chapter were implemented by Qi Han [28]. The design of the solution, methodologies, experiments, results and final metrics were produced by the author of this thesis.

7.1 Algorithms for Face Detection

Face detection is the identification of faces within an image or series of images. It often involves a combination of human motion analysis and skin color analysis [23]. Face detection can be performed based on several clues: skin color (for faces in color images and videos), motion (for faces in videos), facial/head shape, facial appearance, or a combination of these parameters [63]. According to Erik Hjelm [19] the methods for face detection are classified as follows:

1. Feature-based approaches

    • Low-level analysis (edges, gray-levels, color, motion, generalized measure)

    • Feature analysis (feature searching, constellation analysis)

    • Active shape models (snakes, deformable templates)

2. Image based approaches

    • Linear subspace methods

- Neural networks

- Statistical approaches

The first category includes some low-level analysis methods, based on pixel features such as edges, gray information, color information, motion, and generalized measurements. Sub-categories of feature analysis are the feature searching and the constellation analysis; these methods focus on face features such as the eyes. The active shape model is based on local features such as snakes, deformable templates and point distribution models. These kinds of models are statistical models of the shapes of objects that can deform to fit to a new example of the object. The shapes are constrained by a statistical shape model so that they may vary only in ways seen in a training set. The models are usually formed by using principal component analysis to identify the dominant modes of shape variation in observed examples of the shape. Model shapes are formed by linear combinations of the dominant modes [23]. According to Ming-Hsuan Yang et. al. [45] face detection methods are classified into four classes:

1. Knowledge-based methods.

2. Feature invariant approaches

   - Facial features

   - Texture

   - Skin color

   - Multiple features

3. Template matching

   - Predefined face templates

   - Deformable templates

4. Appearance-based method

   - Eigenface

   - Distribution-based

   - Neural network

   - Support Vector Machine (SVM)

   - Naive Bayes Classifier

   - Hidden Markov Model (HMM)

   - Information-Theoretical Approach

In the biometric content analysis the detection of the face is the first challenge. The process of selecting an algorithm is defined by a process presented in Figure 7.1. The first action of the process is the identification and itemization of available algorithms. Every algorithm was programmed and implemented, the algorithms were tested by doing experiments with the

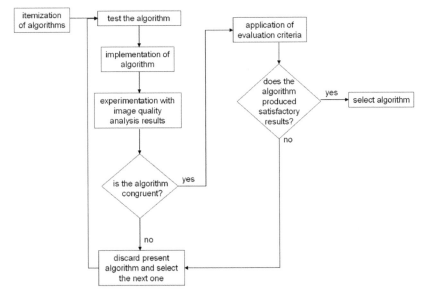

Figure 7.1: Process for Selecting a Face Detection Algorithm

Cualli data set and the results of the implementation were tested with the results obtained in the image quality analysis. The calibration data should be congruent with the results of the implemented face recognition algorithm. It means that an algorithm should be capable to identify the face region of all photographs that conform with the *Cualli data* set using the results produced by the implementation of the image quality analysis. If the algorithm did not work properly for all photographs, it was discarded. The second filter for the algorithm selection is defined for the evaluation criteria where the performance and the exactitude are essential elements. The following methods were implemented to integrate a complete solution for face detection.

7.1.1 The Gray-Level Threshold Method

The image threshold method classifies the pixels of a given image into two classes: those pertaining to an object and those pertaining to the background. The first class includes pixels with gray values that are below or equal to a certain threshold and the second class includes those with gray value above the threshold [69]. The gray-level threshold method was used in the experiments to find the region of the face from a digital passport photo. The intensity of the skin is located in a narrow region of the intensity axis. The pixels are sorted into the two classes by the threshold of the region, see equation 7.1, where th is the threshold, I is the intensity and i, j are the coordinates of intensity axis.

$$I(i,j) = \begin{cases} 255, & \text{if} \quad th_1 < I(i,j) < th_2 \\ 0, & \text{if} \quad I(i,j) < th_1 \quad \text{or} \quad I(i,j) > th_2 \end{cases} \tag{7.1}$$

7.1.1.1 Testing Skin Color Sensitivity

A test with facial images from people with different skin color was performed. The images selected were from people of different races like Caucasian, Asian, African and Amerindo [18]. Figure 7.2 shows some of the original facial images used. The implementation of this method gave sensitive results to the illumination of the facial region and their use with different skin colors derives in variations of the distributions. As it can be seen in Figure 7.3, the results of the intensity quantizing with the threshold are in a range of $(110, 210)$; for the darkest skin color the static range of the intensity was not suitable.

Figure 7.2: Original Images with Different Types of Skin Color

Figure 7.3: Threshold Method without Histogram Equalizing

Conducting a histogram equalization before the quantization can be considered as an improved method. The results are shown in Figure 7.4. The performance for black skin color raises but decreases for the other evaluated skin colors.

7.1.2 Skin Color Based Method

The skin color method is based on the distribution of the skin color in a certain color space. The implemented algorithms are tested in six different color spaces: CIE Lab D65, CIE XYZ-itu D65, Hue saturation brightness, Hue saturation lightness, Hue saturation value and Nor-

Figure 7.4: Threshold Method with Histogram Equalizing

malized RGB. The "Design of Experiments" methodology is applied to the *Cualli data* set to detect the skin color in the color spaces previously mentioned. The objective of this research's phase is to select the color space that best permits to identify the region of the skin and the face features such as eyes region, nose and mouth.

The evaluation of the algorithm is controlled in a matrix called *Achto Cualli Matrix for Face Feature's Identification*. In this matrix the identification of features in a certain color space is qualified with a categorical scale; its values are high, medium and low. This qualification is determined according to the size and resolution of the feature region obtained from white color of the resulting image. Table 7.1 contains the results of the valuation of color spaces and features identification. The skin identification has a high score in all colorspaces. The color space Hue saturation brightness, Hue saturation lightness, Hue saturation value and normalized RGB have the same scoring. The color space that has produced the worst results is CIE Lab D65 and the one that produced the best results is CIE XYZitu D65. In this last color space the regions of hair, skin, eyebrows, eyes and nose are scored as high but the mouth region is scored as medium. In Figures 7.5 and 7.6 the results of skin region detection and the perception of skin, hair, eyebrows, eyes and nose regions in colorspaces CIE Lab and CIE XYZitu are shown. Figures 7.7 and 7.8 show the results of detecting skin region and perception of face features in the colorspaces Hue saturation brightness and Hue saturation lightness. In the experimentation phase one test to evaluate the influence of the colorspace to detect the skin region was performed. Figure 7.9 and Figure 7.10 are examples of the results of detecting skin region and approaches of face features in two colorspaces: Hue saturation value and Normalized RGB. The color space CIE XYZitu D65 obtained the highest scoring in detecting the skin color.

7.1.3   Edge Detecting-Based Method

Edge detection is an image processing operation that computes edge vectors (gradient and orientation) for every point in an image. Edge detection is designated to identify the intensity discontinuity and mark out the object edges. Edge detection is traditionally considered as either a convolution or correlation operation in which each pixel value in the blurred section is replaced with a weighted average of pixels in its neighborhood (including the pixel itself); it is also known as a convolution kernel. Huang et al. [70] classify edge detection algorithms into two classes based on the support of the convolution kernel:

Table 7.1: Example of Results of Experiments from Color Spaces and Features Identification Combination

Feature region	CIE Lab D65	CIE XYZitu D65	Hue saturation brightness	Hue saturation lightness	Hue saturation value	Normalized RGB
Hair	low	high	medium	medium	medium	medium
Skin	high	high	high	high	high	high
Eyebrow	low	high	medium	medium	medium	medium
Eyes	medium	high	medium	medium	medium	medium
Nose	medium	high	medium	medium	medium	high
Mouth	high	medium	high	high	high	high

Figure 7.5: Skin Region Detection in the Colorspace CIE Lab D65

Figure 7.6: Skin Region Detection in the Colorspace CIE XYZitu D65

- With finite support: called mask-based edge detectors because the convolution kernel is with finite support like Sobel, Prewitt, Roberts and Kirsch detectors.

- With infinite support: such as two-dimensional Gaussian detectors like Marr Hildreth and Canny detectors

Figure 7.7: Skin Region Detection in the Colorspace Hue Saturation Brightness

Figure 7.8: Skin Region Detection in the Colorspace Hue Saturation Lightness

Figure 7.9: Skin Region Detection in the Colorspace Hue Saturation Value

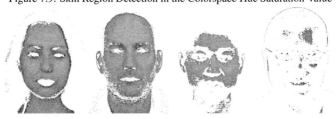

Figure 7.10: Skin Region Detection in the Colorspace RGB

7.1.3.1   Sobel Edge Detector

Edge based methods are suitable for detecting linear features in an image [62]. The Sobel edge detector is based on the Sobel kernel which is a gradient estimation kernel used for edge detection where the horizontal kernel is the convolution of a smoothing filter [23]. The edge region is the place where the linear features are identified. The Sobel operator performs a 2-D spatial gradient measurement on the edge region. It is used to find the approximate absolute gradient magnitude at each point in the input image. The Sobel edge detector uses a pair of $3x3$ convolution masks, one estimates the gradient in the x axis direction and the other estimates the gradient in the y axis direction. Typically a convolution mask is smaller than the input image. As a result, the mask is slid over the image, manipulating a square of pixels at a time [62]. The Sobel masks used are shown in Figure 7.11. The magnitude of the gradient

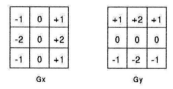

Figure 7.11: Convolution Masks of Sobel Edge Detector

is then calculated using the formula:

$$G = \max(G_x, G_y) \tag{7.2}$$

Where G_x and G_Y are the results of the masking operation on each position.

7.1.3.2   Edge Detection Results

The forms obtained after the edge detection were analyzed and the eyes' edge was discovered. This edge is a distinctive and stable feature that can be used to localize the exact position of the eyes identifying the curve of iris edge. The closed mouth is shown as a rough line. Figure 7.12 shows the eyes and mouth edges detected with the processing of the Soebel detector. These forms can be considered as patterns that could be used for the recognition of the same forms in facial images. Section 7.2 describes the matching algorithms to find the eyes and mouth.

7.1.4   Active Contour Model

The active contour model is also called "snakes", because the deformable contours resemble snakes as they move. It is a combination of deformable model and an algorithm for fitting that model to image data. In one common embodiment the model is a parameterized 2D curve, for example a b-spline parameterized by its control points. Image data, which might be a gradient image or 2D points, induces forces on points on the snake that are translated to forces on the

Figure 7.12: A Result of Edge Detection Implementation

control points or parameters. An iterative algorithm adjusts the control point according to these forces and recomputes them [23]. The active contour model was firstly introduced by Kass et al.[36], deforming a contour to lock onto the features interested in within an image [42]. Given an approximation of the boundary of an object in an image, an active contour model can be used to find the "actual" boundary.

Anyhow an initial guess of the contour should be provided by a user or by another method, possibly an automated one. An active contour is an ordered collection of n points in the image plane:

$$V = \{v_1, \ldots, v_n\}, v_i = (x_i, y_i), \quad i = \{1, \ldots, n\} \qquad (7.3)$$

The point in the contour iteratively approaches the boundary of an object through the solution of an energy minimization problem. For each point in the neighborhood of v_i, an energy term is computed:

$$E_i = \alpha E_{int}(v_i) + \beta E_{ext}(v_i) \qquad (7.4)$$

where $E_{int}(v_i)$ is an energy function dependent on the shape of the contour and $E_{ext}(v_i)$ is an energy function dependent on the image properties such as the gradient, near point v_i. α and β are constants providing the relative weighting of the energy terms. E_i, E_{int} and E_{ext} are matrices. The value at the center of each matrix corresponds to the contour energy at point v_i. Other values in the matrices correspond (spatially) to the energy at each point in the neighborhood of v_i. Each point v_i is moved to the point v_i' corresponding to the location of the minimum value in E_i. This process is illustrated in Figure 7.13, [42]. If the energy functions are chosen correctly, the contour V should approach and stopped at the object boundary.

The energy function E is composed of two parts: the internal energy E_{int} see equation (7.5) and the external energy E_{ext} see equation (7.10). The energy functions are mainly referred to [42]; nevertheless some theoretical analysis and testing in the program implemented conduced to modify and simplify the formulae of the energy functions.

The internal energy function is defined as follows:

$$\alpha E_{int}(v_i) = c E_{con}(v_i) + b E_{bal}(v_i) \qquad (7.5)$$

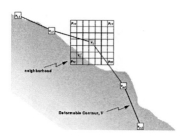

Figure 7.13: The Movement of a Snake

where $E_{con}(v_i)$ is the continuity energy that enforces the shape of the contour and $E_{bal}(v_i)$ is a balloon force that causes the contour to grow (balloon) or shrink. c and b provide the relative weighting of the energy terms. In the absence of other influences, the continuity energy term coerces an open deformable contour into a straight line and a closed deformable contour into a circle. The energy term for each element $e_{jk}(v_i)$ in the matrix $E_{con}(v_i)$ is defined as follows:

$$e_{jk}(v_i) = \|p_{jk}(v_i) - \gamma(v_{i-1} + v_{i+1})\|^2 \qquad (7.6)$$

where $p_{jk}(v_i)$ is the point in the image that corresponds spatially to energy element $e_{jk}(v_i)$ $\gamma = 0.5$ for an open contour. In this case, the minimum energy point is the point exactly half way between v_{i-1} and v_{i+1}. For the case of a closed contour, V is given a modulus of n. Therefore, $v_{n+i} = v_i$ γ is then defined as follows:

$$\gamma = \frac{1}{2 \cos(\frac{2\pi}{n})} \qquad (7.7)$$

Here, the point of minimum energy of $E_{con}(v_i)$ is pushed outward so that V becomes a circle [42]. This behavior is illustrated in Figure 7.14 [42] .

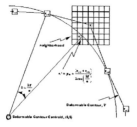

Figure 7.14: The Movement of a Point due to Continuity Energy

A balloon force can be used on a closed deformable contour to force the contour to expand (or shrink) in the absence of external influences. A contour initialized within an uniform image object will expand under the influence of a balloon force until it nears the object boundary (at which point the external energy function affects its motion). Figure 7.15 [42] illustrates this

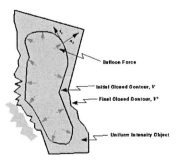

Figure 7.15: The Movement of a Point due to Balloon Energy

behavior. Chalana et al. suggest an adaptive balloon force that varies inversely proportional to the image gradient magnitude [67]. The adaptive balloon force is strong in homogeneous regions and weak near object boundaries, edges, and lines. The energy term for each element $e_{jk}(v_i)$ in the matrix $\boldsymbol{E}_{bal}(v_i)$ is expressed as a dot product:

$$e_{jk}(v_i) = n_i \bullet (v_i - p_{jk}(v_i)) \tag{7.8}$$

where n_i is the outward unit normal of $\boldsymbol{V}$ at point v_i and $p_{jk}(v_i)$ is the point in the neighborhood of v_i corresponding to entry $e_{jk}(v_i)$ in the energy matrix. Therefore, the balloon energy is lowest at points farthest from v_i in the direction of n_i. n_i can be found by rotating the tangent vector t_i by 90°. t_i is easily computed:

$$t_i = \frac{v_i - v_{i-1}}{\|v_i - v_{i-1}\|} + \frac{v_{i+1} - v_i}{\|v_{i+1} - v_i\|} \tag{7.9}$$

So n_i is a unit vector normal to t_i. The external energy function attracts the deformable contour to interesting features such as object boundaries in an image. Any energy expression that accomplishes this attraction can be considered for use. Here the external energy function is expressed as follows:

$$\beta \boldsymbol{E}_{ext}(v_i) = m \boldsymbol{E}_{mag}(v_i) + g \boldsymbol{E}_{grad}(v_i) \tag{7.10}$$

where $\boldsymbol{E}_{ext}(v_i)$ is an expression that attracts the contour to high or low intensity regions and $\boldsymbol{E}_{grad}(v_i)$ is an energy term that moves the contour towards edges. Again the constants m and g are provided to adjust the relative weights of the terms.
Each element in the intensity energy matrix $\boldsymbol{E}_{mag}(v_i)$ is assigned to the intensity value of the corresponding image point in the neighborhood of v_i:

$$e_{jk}(v_i) = I(p_{jk}(v_i)) \tag{7.11}$$

Then, if m is positive, the contour is attracted to regions of low intensity and vice-versa. The image gradient energy function attracts the deformable contour to edges in the image. An energy expression proportional to the gradient magnitude will attract the contour to any edge:

$$e_{jk}(v_i) = -|\nabla I(p_{jk}(v_i))| \tag{7.12}$$

When active contours are used to find object boundaries, an energy expression that discriminates between edges of adjacent is desirable. The key to such an expression is that the gradients at the edges of the objects have different directions. Further, the direction of the gradient at the object's edge should be similar to the direction of the unit normal of the contour. This situation is illustrated in Figure 7.16 [42]. The value for each element in the directional gradi-

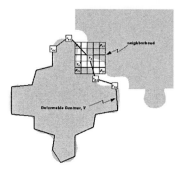

Figure 7.16: The Movement of a Point due to Gradient Energy

ent energy matrix $E_{grad}(v_i)$ can therefore be defined by a dot product between the unit normal of the deformable contour and the image gradient:

$$e_{jk}(v_i) = -n_i \bullet \bigtriangledown I(p_{jk}(v_i)) \tag{7.13}$$

where n_i is the unit normal of the contour at point v_i. The energy functions introduced in the previous section should be scaled in the way, that the neighborhood matrices contain comparable values. This process is referred to as regularization. Here each of the energy functions is adjusted to the range $[0, 1]$. At each point in the deformable contour, the elements in neighborhood matrix for the continuity energy are simply scaled to the range $[0, 1]$:

$$e'_{jk}(v_i) = \frac{e_{jk}(v_i) - e_{min}(v_i)}{e_{max}(v_i) - e_{min}(v_i)} \tag{7.14}$$

where $e_{min}(v_i)$ and $e_{max}(v_i)$ are the minimum and maximum valued elements, respectively, in $E_{con}(v_i)$. Similarly, the balloon energy, intensity energy and the gradient energy are scaled to the range $[0, 1]$ applying Formula 7.14

The first results of the snake method are shown in Figure 7.17. The performance of the snake is influenced by the constant in equation (7.5) and equation 7.10. So the selecting of the constant and the optimizing of the energy function still needs some other efforts.

The results of this experimentation phase conduce to conclude that there are three main disadvantages in the use of the active contour model: firstly, it is slow for the numerous searching loops; secondly, the algorithm achieved was not stable on extracting the face from different images; thirdly, because of the influence of other features like hair, shadows, beard, the contour of faces usually is an irregular closed curve that does not help to measure the attributes of the features (see Figure 7.17). The active contour model method has demonstrated not to

Figure 7.17: The Contour of a Face found by Snake

be an optimal choice to detect the face. The skin color model based method and edge detecting based method achieve the face detection and feature extraction. The gray-level threshold method helps to find the background region. The active contour model method was given up considering the computing speed and the efficiency. Edge detection results can be used to localize the exact position of the eyes and mouth. The selected methods for face detection used in this thesis are:

1. Gray-level threshold

2. Skin color mode-based

3. Edge detecting-based

4. Active contour model (snake)

7.2   Detection of Facial Image Features

In this thesis a facial image feature is considered as a distinctive part of a digital passport photo such as background, head, face, eyes, mouth and resolution. Facial image feature detection is the location of features, normally performed after face detection although it can be used as part of face detection. The process of feature detection is performed systematically, it begins with a detector that identifies the feature and evaluates if the detection was successful or not. The first feature to detect is the region of the eyes. There is a relationship of eyes' region and the mouth position. According to [14] some of the measurements are paired, when there is a corresponding measurement on the left and right side of the face. Following that principle and doing some analogies with the facial anthropometrics, the detection of facial features such as eyes and mouth corners is done. The model followed to detect facial features is presented in Figure 7.18. The background and the eyes region are simultaneously detected. The eyes region are key features to find the localization of the mouth region, there is a correspondent anthropometry that defines the relationship with the left and right corners of the mouth with the middle point of both eyes. Once the mouth region is located, the face region and the head region are detected simultaneously using as reference points for their areas the coordinates of eyes and mouth.

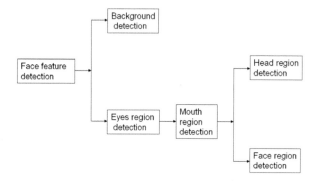

Figure 7.18: Model Followed to Detect Facial Features

7.2.1 Background Detection

The background is the area of a facial image behind the individual's head (foreground), the identification of the background is done using the Gray-Level Threshold Method. The usefulness of this method was discovered after the experimentation phase detailed in section 7.1.1. The algorithm to detect the background designed by Qi Han [28] is compound of the following procedures:

1. Conversion of the color image I_c to the gray-level image I_g

2. Segmentation of the gray-level image I_g with two thresholds of gray-level which distinguish the background, hair and face

3. Filling the background region with gray color

4. Identification of the gray color from the gray-level segmented image I_s

5. Identification of background region with another color

The algorithm is implemented and demonstrated with Figure 7.19. From left to right are shown the original color image I_c, the gray-level image I_g, the segmented image I_s and the result of background detection I_b. The algorithm's validation was done using the *Achto Cualli Dataset* and the different subsets to test the results' congruency with the conclusions previously specified. This section describes the relevant results generated.

Figure 7.19: Results of the Background Detection Process

7.2.2   Eyes Region Detection

Eyes are determinant features to distinguish an image from a facial image. The eyes' position is the most important information to evaluate a facial image and to detect the rest of the facial features because of the geometric relationships between each others [11]. Many features' rough positions or regions could be deduced. A two-stage template matching method to find the accurate positions of the eyes is developed. The algorithm to detect the eyes designed by Qi Han [28] is compound of the following procedures:

1. Segmentation of the skin region I_s from the original color image

2. Conversion of the skin color detection result I_s to a gray-level image I_{sg}

3. Conversion of I_{sg} to a binary image I_{sgb} and then use the morphology open and close operation to eliminate the noise points

4. Matching the result image I'_{sgb} with a template of both eyes and eyebrows, compute the correlation value and select the greatest value, the corresponding position is supposed to be the center of the eyes template, then the eyes band is found.

5. In the small region of eyes band, search for the irises by an iris edge template. The search is implemented on the corresponding region of an edge detection result

Patterns for the eyes region including eyebrows were designed by Qi Han [28] to identify the eyes region. These patterns were created after the analysis of different features manually extracted to conform a multiformed figure. Figure 7.20 shows the pattern of region of eyes including the eyebrow. A pattern for iris detection was also created, Figure 7.21 shows the pattern for iris identification.

7.2.3   Mouth Region Detection

As mentioned in section 7.1.3.2, it was discovered that applying the edge algorithm to a facial image the mouth is shown as a rough line as can be seen in Figure 7.12. The detection of the

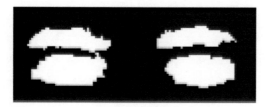

Figure 7.20: Region of Eyes Pattern

Figure 7.21: Iris Pattern

mouth is done through the corners of the mouth identification using a pattern to match every corner of the mouth. Figure 7.22 shows the template to match the left end point of the mouth, since there is a *parity* of the right with the left side of the face, right and left corner of the mouth are detected with similar patterns.

The algorithm to find the mouth is:

1. Mark the region of the mouth, based on the position of the eyes and the geometric relations of the facial features, mark the approximate region of the mouth

2. Extract the edge region of this region

3. Match the templates with the mouth edge region, and find the corner of the mouth

4. Based on the end point of mouth, mark the region of mouth

Figure 7.22: Patterns to Find the Mouth Region

7.2.4   Face Region Detection

The face region is detected using the skin color result explained in section 7.1 and using the landmarks of eyes region and mouth. Knowing the landmarks and the geometric relation of face features, the face region can be identified.

7.2.5 Head Region Detection

The head region is identified in a rectangle that is drawn after the identification of the other features. Figure 7.23

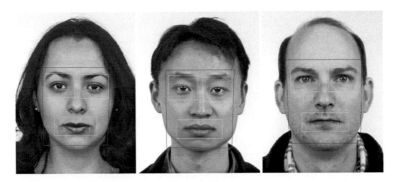

Figure 7.23: Examples of the Results Generate for Facial Features Detection

7.3 Ground Truth of Biometric Content

The validity of biometric content according to the specification of the standard [4] consists of the individual's head and face regions distribution on the sample to be evaluated. Figure 7.24 shows a portrait image and head outline to display dimensions A, B, BB, CC, and DD. Where:

- AA represents an imaginary vertical line positioned at the horizontal center of the image. It symbolizes the approximate horizontal midpoints of the mouth and of the bridge of the nose.

- BB denotes the vertical distance from the bottom edge of the image of an imaginary horizontal line passing through the center of the eyes. It shall be between 50% and 70% of the total vertical length B of the image.

- CC defines the head width considered as the horizontal distance between the midpoints of two imaginary vertical lines; each imaginary line is drawn between the upper and lower lobes of each ear and shall be positioned where the external ear connects to the head.

- DD represents the length of a head which is defined as the vertical distance between the base of the chin and the crown.

The algorithms implemented in this thesis are based on the position of eyes and mouth. Many features of the facial image can be derived. Before measurement of the features, the geometric

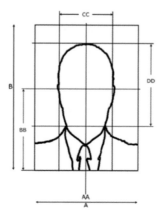

Figure 7.24: Geometric Characteristics of the Full Frontal Face Image

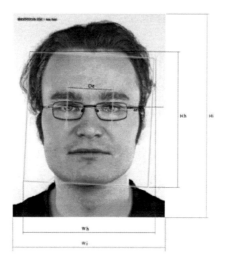

Figure 7.25: Expression of Features

parameters of feature points should be expressed into the description of the features of the facial image. The parameters of the features are defined as shown in Figure 7.25, the parameters are defined in the Table 7.2:

The biometric content attributes to be evaluated are head pose angle, width of head, length of head, number of faces, horizontally centered face, vertical position of the face, resolution

Table 7.2: Biometric Parameters of Features

Variable	Meaning
D_e	The distance between the two eyes
a_e	The angle between the line connect two eyes and the horizontal line
W_h	The width of the head
W_i	The width of the image
H_h	The height of the head
H_i	The height of the image
N_f	The number of faces
C_{ex}	The distance between the left edge of the image and the vertical line which across the center point between the two eyes
C_{ey}	The distance between the bottom edge of the image and the horizontal line which across the center point between the two eyes

of the head and eyes center. Table 7.3 and 7.4 show the conformance attributes and the mathematical expressions of the features restrictions. They are considered as constraints or conformance conditions.

For biometric content an attribute of features can be qualified as acceptable (true or 1) if its geometric data are in the specified interval. In other cases it is qualified as unacceptable (false or 0).

7.4 Summary

In this chapter the different algorithms for face and features detection are explained. The experimentation phase was applied for the *Achto Cualli Dataset* to test the performance and results of the algorithms. The results of the experimentation conduce to conclude that there are three main disadvantages in the application of the active contour model: first, it is slow for the numerous searching loops; second, the algorithm achieved was not stable on extracting the face from different images; third, because of the influence of other features like hair, shadows, beard, the contour of the face usually is an irregular closed curve which does not help to measure the attributes of the features as can be seen in Figure 7.17. The active contour model method has shown weaknesses to find the face. The skin color model based method and edge detecting based method achieve the face detection and feature extraction. The gray-level threshold method helps to find the background region, while the active contour model method was given up considering the computing speed and the efficiency. Edge detection results can be used to localize the exact position of the eyes and mouth. The selected methods for face

Table 7.3: Biometric Conformance Attributes

ID	Attribute	Condition
APA	Head pose angle	less than +/-5 degree
WAH	Width of head	great than 5/7 of width of image
LOH	Length of head	no more than 80% of the vertical length
NRF	Number of faces	only one
HCF	Horizontally centered face	lies on the vertical line at horizontal center
VP	Vertical position	between 50% and 70%
RSL	Resolution	at least 180 pixels of resolution for the width of the head
DCE	Distance between center of both eyes	roughly 90 pixels from eye center to eye center

Table 7.4: Biometric Conformance Mathematical Expressions

ID	Expression
APA	$a_e < 5$
WAH	$W_h/W_i > 5/7$
LOH	$H_h < H_i \times 80\%$
NRF	—
HCF	$C_{ex} = W_i/2$
VP	$30\% < \frac{C_{ey}}{H_i < 50}\%$
RSL	$W_i >= 180$
DCE	$D_e <= 90$

detection used in this thesis are:

1. Gray-level threshold

2. Skin color mode-based

3. Edge detecting-based

4. Active contour model (snakes)

A combination of those algorithms was used to detect the face features. The validation of the biometric content of a facial image is determined for the constraints specified in the ISO standard [4] and presented in Table 7.3 and Table 7.4.

Chapter 8

Development of Metrics for the Calculation of Digital Passport Photographs' Quality

A passport photograph contains some attributes which have a high influence on its perception[37]. The influence attributes identified in the conformance requirements of the international standards [48] and [4] are categorized into three groups:

- *Photograph requirements* for the process of taking the photographs with certain specifications. They also promote the interoperability and open interchange between photograph and individual.

- *Image requirements* according to Keelan [37] are attributes contributing to the perceived image quality. They are defined in a broad sense, for example unsharpness, contrast, brightness, lighting quality and color balance.

- *Biometric requirements* are included attributes such as head pose angle, width of head, length of head, number of faces, horizontally centered face, vertical position, resolution and distance between center of both eyes.

In a 2D (two dimensional) image such as a digital passport photograph, the image processing highly depends on the image's quality. The image's quality is always affected by the environment for example by illumination [39]. It can be difficult to detect a 2D face feature in various poses or expressions because some features might vanish [39]. Digital passport photographs quality can not be quantified by a single metric and quality measures should be calculated without any reference image. Following that principle the solution proposed in this thesis consists of: The analysis and quantification of the terms "good" or "bad" quality introducing scale values for photograph, image and biometric attributes and the determination of a ground truth which serves as criterion of goodness or badness to qualify a photograph.

8.1 Assignment of Weights to Quality Attributes

Quality attributes were extracted from the international standards documents [48] and [4] and were classified into different subsets as presented in Chapter 4. The main set of quality attributes is formed by three subsets of attributes: photograph, image and biometric quality attributes. The main set of quality attributes is defined as set A, which originally is integrated by twentyseven elements, however it is proposed in this thesis to consider thirty elements adding image width and image height each as one attribute instead of image size; the other two attributes to add are impulsive noise and blur noise. These quality attributes are described and analized in Chapter 6. The set A is defined as follows:

- A = {expression, red eye, head, background, size (image width, image height), antiquity, vertical position, no flash reflection, width of head, horizontally centered face, resolution, brightness, impulsive noise, blur noise, length of head, head pose angle, contrast, focus, lighting scene, dermis, eyes, facing, percentage, exposure, mouth, color, file type, number of faces and distance between center of both eyes}

The set A of quality attributes is integrated by subsets P, I and B, where subset P contains the Photograph quality attributes, subset I contains Image quality attributes and subset B is formed by Biometric quality attributes:

- P = {antiquity, size (image width, image height), focus, kighting scene, dermis, background, eyes, facing, head, percentage, exposure, expression, mouth, no flash reflection}

- I = {brightness, contrast, color, red eye, file type, blur noise, impulsive noise}

- B = {head pose angle, length of head, width of head, number of faces, horizontally centered face, vertical position, resolution, distance between center of both eyes}

In the specifications of quality attributes of a digital passport photograph, it is not established which attribute or attributes are most important. There is no guide to know in which order the quality attributes should be evaluated. Assigning priorities or precedences arbitrarily for an attribute can influence the results of a quality metric. A solution of this problem is to assign a weight to each attribute considering the opinion of Technical User Experts (TUE) and Practial User Experts (PUE) which have been surveyed as explained in Chapter 5. They have experience in working directly or indirectly with face images in their daily activities and the use of some kind of normative documents to perform their activities. The international survey methodology and results are explained in Chapter 5.

A weight for an attribute is defined considering it as part of the main set and as part of the corresponding subset as well as considering the relevance obtained from the opinion of Technical User Experts and Practical User Experts as explained in Chapter 5 in Table 5.13. Considering that the main set A has originally twentyseven elements, an attribute x has the share value $s = \frac{1}{27} = 0.037037$. The weight W for attribute x considering the relevance obtained from the meaning of Technical User Experts is defined by Formula 8.1.

$$W_x(TUE) = r(TUE) \cdot s(A) \qquad (8.1)$$

$$W_x(PUE) = r(PUE) \cdot s(A) \qquad (8.2)$$

In Formula 8.1 $r(TUE)$ is the relevance obtained from the meaning of Technical User Experts, in Formula 8.2 in both Formulas $s(A)$ represents the share value (0.037037) for attribute x considering it as part of the main set A.

Applying both formulas to all original attributes, the values obtained according to the relevance are the same but the order of the attributes varies depending on the opinions of the different kind of experts. The results are presented in Table 8.1.

Table 8.1: Weight of Attributes According to Technical User Experts and Practial User Experts (1/2)

Relevance	Weight	Attribute (TUE)	Attribute (PUE)
27	1	Expression	Head
26	0.9629629	No Red Eye	Brightness
25	0.9259259	Head	Size
24	0.8888888	Background	Contrast
23	0.8518518	Size	Antiquity
22	0.8148148	Antiquity	Expression
21	0.7777777	Vertical Position of Eyes	Horizontally Centered Face
20	0.7407407	No Flash Reflection	Width of Head
19	0.7037037	Width of Head	Background
18	0.6666666	Horizontally Centered Face	Head Pose Angle
17	0.6296296	Resolution	No Flash Reflection

The weight values presented in Tables 8.1 and 8.2 are used to calculate the weights of the attributes' subsets. The value of an attribute should be calculated according to the subset it pertains. This calculation permits a more exact quality measurement because if the sense weight to be considered comes from the main set, it could mean that all attributes presented are measurable. In this thesis in Chapter 4 every attribute is analyzed, as result of this analysis the hypothesis *not all attributes specified are measurable* was generated. In Chapter 6 and Chapter 7 the implementation of different algorithms to measure quality attributes from different categories is described. Under this precedent a new weights' calculation based on the user expert's weight was obtained as well as the share value of the attribute as member of a subset of quality attributes measured in the development of this thesis.

A new formula is applied to each subset, for example in Formula 8.3 the considered subset is P which represents the Photograph quality attributes. The weight $W_x(TUE)$ corresponds to the

Table 8.2: Weight of Attributes According to Technical User Experts and Practial User Experts (2/2)

Relevance	Weight	Attribute (TUE)	Attribute (PUE)
16	0.5925925	Brightness	Resolution
15	0.5555555	Length of Head	Vertical Position
14	0.5185185	Head Pose Angle	Red Eye
13	0.4814814	Contrast	Length of Head
12	0.4444444	Focus	Focus
11	0.4074074	Lighting Scene	Lighting Scene
10	0.3703703	Dermis	Dermis
9	0.3333333	Eyes	Eyes
8	0.2962962	Facing	Facing
7	0.2592592	Percentage	Percentage
6	0.2222222	Exposure	Exposure
5	0.1851851	Mouth	Mouth
4	0.1481481	Color	Color
3	0.1111111	File type	File type
2	0.0740740	Number of Faces	Number of Faces
1	0.0370370	Distance between Center of Both Eyes	Distance between Center of Both Eyes

calculated weight for the attribute x considering it as member of the main set A. This subset is originally integrated by fourteen attributes, nevertheless it has fifteen: the attribute Size is integrated by two elements: image's width and image's height. The subset of photograph attributes measured is compound of three measurable attributes: image width, image height and identification of background. In Formula 8.3 the share value of each subset's element $s(P)$ is 0.3333333

$$W_x P(TUE) = W_x(TUE) \cdot s(P) \tag{8.3}$$

$$W_x P(PUE) = W_x(PUE) \cdot s(P) \tag{8.4}$$

In Formula 8.3 $W_x P(TUE)$ is the calculated weight according to Technical User Experts opinion for an attribute x of the subset P, $W_x(TUE)$ is the calculated weight according to Technical User Experts obtained with Formula 8.1, and $s(P)$ is the share value 0.3333333 obtained, considering that subset P has three measured elements. Formula 8.4 defines the calculation of the weight for photograph attributes' subset considering the opinion of Practical User Experts; it is defined by $W_x P(PUE)$ for an attribute x of the subset P. $W_x(PUE)$

is the calculated weight according to Practical User Experts obtained with Formula 8.2, and $s(P)$ is the share value 0.3333333 obtained considering that subset P has three measured elements.

The results of application of the Formulas 8.3 and 8.4 for photograph quality attributes are presented in Table 8.3.

Table 8.3: Weight of Photograph Quality Attributes According to Technical User Experts and Practial User Experts

Attribute	Weight (A) (TUE)	Weight (P) (TUE)	Weight (A) (PUE)	Weight (P) (PUE)
Image width	0.4259259	0.1419753	0.4629630	0.1543210
Image height	0.4259259	0.1419753	0.4629630	0.1543210
Background identifiable	0.88888889	0.2962963	0.7037040	0.2345680
$\sum$	1.740740741	0.5802469	1.6296300	0.5432100

The original subset of image quality attributes is formed by seven attributes: brightness, contrast, color, red eye, file type, blur noise, impulsive noise. The subset I of measured attributes is compound by five attributes: brightness, contrast, file type, blur noise and impulsive noise. In Formula 8.5 the share value of each subset's element $s(I)$ is 0.2000000.

$$W_x I(TUE) = W_x(TUE) \cdot s(I) \tag{8.5}$$

$$W_x I(PUE) = W_x(PUE) \cdot s(I) \tag{8.6}$$

In Formula 8.5 $W_x I(TUE)$ is the calculated weight according to Technical User Experts opinion for an attribute x of the subset I, $W_x(TUE)$ is the calculated weight according to Technical User Experts obtained with Formula 8.1, and $s(I)$ is the share value 0.2000000 obtained, considering that subset I has five measured elements. Formula 8.6 defines the calculation of the weight for photograph attributes' subset considering the opinion of Practical User Experts. It is represented by $W_x I(PUE)$ and it is the calculated weight according to Practical User Experts opinion for an attribute x of the subset I, $W_x(TUE)$ is the calculated weight according to Technical User Experts obtained with Formula 8.1. The share value is the same as the used in Formula 8.1 obtained considering that subset I has five measured elements.

The results of application of the Formulas 8.5 and 8.6 for image quality attributes are presented in Table 8.4.
The original set of biometric quality attributes is composed by eight attributes: pose angle, width of head, length of head, horizontally centered face, vertical position of the eyes, resolu-

Table 8.4: Weight of Image Quality Attributes According to Technical User Experts and Practial User Experts

Attribute	Weight (A) (TUE)	Weight (I) (TUE)	Weight (A) (PUE)	Weight (I) (PUE)
Brightness	0.5925926	0.1185185	0.9629630	0.1925926
Contrast	0.4814815	0.0962963	0.8888890	0.1777778
File type	0.1111111	0.0222222	0.1111111	0.0222222
Blur noise	0	0	0	0
Impulsive noise	0	0	0	0
$\sum$	1.1851852	0.2370370	1.9629630	0.3925926

tion, number of faces. The subset B of measured attributes is compound by the eight attributes mentioned before. In Formula 8.7 the share value of each subset´s element $s(B)$ is 0.1250000.

$$W_x B(TUE) = W_x(TUE) \cdot s(B) \qquad (8.7)$$

$$W_x B(PUE) = W_x(PUE) \cdot s(B) \qquad (8.8)$$

In Formula 8.7 the weight $W_x B(TUE)$ is the calculated weight according to Technical User Experts opinion for an attribute x of the subset B, $W_x(TUE)$ is the calculated weight according to Technical User Experts obtained with Formula 8.1, and sB is the share value 0.1250000 obtained, considering that subset B has five measured elements. The Formula 8.8 defines the calculation of the weight for photograph attributes' subset considering the opinion of Practical User Experts, where $W_x B(PUE)$ is the calculated weight according to Practical User Experts opinion for an attribute x of the subset B, $W_x(PUE)$ is the calculated weight according to Technical User Experts obtained with Formula 8.1, and $s(B)$ is the same share value as the one used in Formula 8.7.

The results of application of the formulas 8.7 and 8.8 for biometric quality attributes are presented in Table 8.5.

8.2   Conventional Quality Index

A conventional quality index has a single value determined through objective means from attributes of quality within a digital passport photograph accounting for its viewing conditions and the properties of the human visual system [76]. In this section the calculi of three quality indices are obtained: for photograph quality attributes, for image quality attributes and for biometric attributes. The indices produced are results of the evaluation of the *Cualli dataset* whose values are interpreted as calibration values for digital passport photographs for people with caucasian characteristics.

Table 8.5: Weight of Biometric Quality Attributes According to Technical User Experts and Practial User Experts

Attribute	Weight (A) (TUE)	Weight (B) (TUE)	Weight (A) (PUE)	Weight (B) (PUE)
Pose angle	0.5185185	0.0648148	0.6666670	0.0833334
Width of head	0.7037037	0.0879630	0.7407410	0.0925926
Length of head	0.7037037	0.0879630	0.4814810	0.0601851
Horizontally centered face	0.6666667	0.0833333	0.7777780	0.0972223
Vertical position (position of eyes)	0.7777778	0.0972222	0.5555560	0.0694445
Distance between center of both eyes	0.0370370	0.0046296	0.0370370	0.0046296
Resolution	0.6296296	0.0787037	0.5925930	0.0740741
Number of faces	0.0740741	0.0092593	0.0740740	0.0092593
$\sum$	4.1111111	0.5138889	3.925927	0.4907409

8.2.1 Photograph Attributes Quality Index

The Photograph Attributes Quality Index (PAQI) is integrated by the cumulative addition of the weights plus the corresponding fraction value of the measured photograph quality attributes such as: image width, image height and identification of background. The weights are presented in Table 8.3, the first calculation of PAQI is expressed by Formula (8.9), where the cumulative addition holds just the share value s of the respective attribute i that accomplish the related constraint.

$$PAQI = \sum_{i=1}^{n} s_i \qquad (8.9)$$

Formula (8.10) expresses the calculation of PAQI(TUE) where the cumulative addition holds just the share value of the respective attribute that accomplish the related constraint.

$$PAQI(TUE) = \sum_{i=1}^{n} W_i(TUE) \qquad (8.10)$$

Where $W_i(TUE)$ is the weight of the attribute defined in Formula 8.3 applying the relevance assigned by the Technical User Experts and i controls the contribution of every attribute that accomplishes the related constraint.

In the same way Formula (8.11) expresses the calculation PAQI(PUE), where $W_i(PUE)$ is the weight of the attribute defined in Formula 8.4 and presented in Table 8.6 applying the rele-

Table 8.6: Parameters to Calculate the Photograph Attribute Quality Index

Attribute	Constraint	s(P)	W (TUE)	W (PUE)
Image width	$W \geq 240 pixels$	0.3333333	0.0648148	0.0833334
Image height	$H \geq 320 pixels$	0.3333333	0.0879630	0.0925926
Background identifiable	0 if segmentation was not done	0.3333333	0.0879630	0.0601851
$\sum$		1	1.7407407	0.5802469

vance assigned by the Practical User Experts and i controls the contribution of every attribute that accomplishes the corresponding constraint.

$$PAQI(PUE) = \sum_{i=1}^{n} W_i(PUE) \qquad (8.11)$$

An optimal quality is achieved if all the measured photograph quality attributes fullfil the constraints. The optimal values of PAQI are $PAQI = 1$, $PAQI(TUE) = 1.7407407$ and $PAQI(PUE) = 0.5802469$. When a calculated value of PAQI for a desired digital passport photograph results smaller than one of the optimal values of PAQI it is assumed that there is missing one or more attributes that did not accomplish the quality constraints.

8.2.2   Image Attributes Quality Index

The Image Attributes Quality Index (IAQI) is defined by the addition of contrast and brightness values subtracting the addition of impulsive noise and blurring. Noise and blurring are deviations of a signal away from its "true" value [23]. Any value obtained from their addition should be subtracted from the result of the addition of contrast and brightness to warrant an index with "true" values of the signals. The values of image quality attributes of the *Cualli datastet* were calculated for different colorspaces and types of file (compressed and uncompressed). The value of IAQI must indicate how "good" or how "bad" the image attributes of an evaluated facial image are. The determination of the acceptance is given by a range of acceptance of the image attributes in Table 8.7. Parameter $\bar{x}$ represents the arithmetic mean of a certain attribute in a certain colorspace, T determines the optimal value obtained for an attribute and its calculation varies according to the related attribute. Both parameters were calculated for the *Cualli dataset* for different types of files. The interval values obtained for every attribute determine the acceptance threshold of "good" quality. The details of those calculi are explained in Chapter 6.

Once it was verified a photograph has accurate values of contrast, brightness, impulsive noise and blur noise, an index to represent the quality of image attributes can be calculated. This index is expresed as follows:

$$IAQI = C + B - (IN + BN) \qquad (8.12)$$

Table 8.7: Image Attributes Quality Constraints

Attribute	Calculated Parameters	Condition
Contrast	$\overline{x}_c, T_c$	$T_c > \overline{x}_c$
Brightness	$\overline{x}_b, T_b$	$T_b \leq \overline{x}_b$
Impulsive Noise	$\overline{x}_{in}, T_{in}$	$\overline{x}_{in} \leq T_{in}$
Blur Noise	$\overline{x}_{bn}, T_{bn}$	$\overline{x}_{bn} \leq T_{bn}$

where IAQI means Image Attributes Quality Index, C is the calculated contrast value, B is the calculated brightness value, IN is the value of impulsive noise and BN is the value of blur noise. The index represents the result of the addition of contrast value plus brightness value minus the addition of impulsive noise´s value plus blur noise's value.

Other indices to represent the quality of image attributes can be defined applying the weight values obtained from the opinion of Technical User Experts and Practical User Experts for every attribute to the index defined in Formula 8.12. The use of a weight for a certain attribute determines the precedence or importance an attribute has and it works as factor that adds a higher or lower value to the attribute according to it's relevance. The Image Attributes Quality Index (IAQI) for TUE or PUE applying the weights for every kind of experts can be defined as presented in Formulas 8.13 and 8.14 respectively.

$$IAQI(TUE) = C \cdot W_C(TUE) + B \cdot W_B(TUE) - (IN + BN) + W_{FT}(TUE) \quad (8.13)$$

$$IAQI(PUE) = C \cdot W_C(PUE) + B \cdot W_B(PUE) - (IN + BN) + W_{FT}(PUE) \quad (8.14)$$

In Formulas 8.13 and 8.14 the calculi of IAQI values have almost the same parameters, the variation is given by the group of experts taken into account (TUE or PUE). In both Formulas C is the calculated contrast value, B is the calculated brightness value, IN is the value of impulsive noise and BN is the value of blur noise. $W_C(TUE)$ is the weight defined for contrast value according to TUE opinion obtained from Table 8.4, $W_B(TUE)$ is the weight defined for brightness value according TUE opinion obtained from Table 8.4, $W_{FT}(TUE)$ is the weight calculated for the file type attribute, $W_C(PUE)$ is the weight defined for contrast value according to PUE opinion obtained from Table 8.4, $W_B(PUE)$ is the weight defined for brightness value according PUE opinion obtained from Table 8.4, $W_{FT}(TUE)$ is the weight calculated for the file type attribute, the weight of W_{FT} will be added just if the file type to be analyzed is compressed in format JPG as specified in document of international standards [48], [4].

The results are considered as the calibration values of the IAQI in its different alternatives of calculi. The calibration values are presented for compressed files in Table 8.8 and for uncompressed files in Table 8.9.

Table 8.8: Calibration Values of Image Attribute Quality Index for Compressed Files

Colorspace	IAQI	IAQI (T)	IAQI (TUE)	IAQI (T) (TUE)	IAQI (PUE)	IAQI (T) (PUE)
CIE Lab D65	0.825635	0.980863	0.119352	0.133106	0.180781	0.207945
CIE XYZ D65	0.663227	0.903392	0.099220	0.119546	0.148896	0.189803
Hue saturation brightness	0.656439	0.864223	0.098499	0.119441	0.147641	0.185273
Hue saturation lightness	0.669172	0.862424	0.100029	0.119172	0.150108	0.184889
Hue saturation value	0.777363	0.866779	0.113082	0.119738	0.171098	0.185772
Normalized RGB	0.656109	1.381606	0.098521	0.1690088	0.147668	0.277014

Table 8.9: Calibration Values of Image Attributes Quality Index for Uncompressed Files

Colorspace	IAQI	IAQI (T)	IAQI (TUE)	IAQI (T) (TUE)	IAQI (PUE)	IAQI (T) (PUE)
CIE Lab D65	0.795195	1.294168	0.071217	0.167360	0.130400	0.266567
CIE XYZitu D65	0.644869	0.673700	0.052645	0.101457	0.100927	0.159001
Hue saturation brightness	0.641317	1.060559	0.051951	0.142275	0.099910	0.222761
Hue saturation lightness	0.678460	0.879085	0.056488	0.120457	0.107309	0.187608
Hue saturation value	0.779935	0.852469	0.068908	0.117973	0.127114	0.182915
Normalized RGB	0.663633	0.876518	0.054723	0.120084	0.104447	0.187060

The ground truth presented in Tables 8.8 and 8.9 represents the ranges of acceptance of an IAQI calculated for a desired photograph if the evaluated photograph is a compressed file, the reference values to be used are from Table 8.8, the value of the new index calculated should be between IAQI and IAQI(T). The difference between the ranges of IAQI and IAQI(TUE) or IAQI(PUE) indicates that the range of quality validated for the user-experts group is shorter because it takes attributes' parameters more exact into account.

8.2.3   Biometric Attributes Quality Index

The Biometric Attributes Quality Index (BAQI) represents values from attributes specified in the international standards [48], [4]. The *Achto Pohua* methodology was implemented in Chapter 7 to determine the quality of the biometric content. The result obtained is a constrained ground truth which must be accomplished by the measurement of facial image's geometric information such as head pose angle, width and length of head, number of faces, horizontally centered face, vertical position and resolution.

The BAQI must express a value that indicates how "good" or how "bad" the biometric attributes of an evaluated facial image are. The concept "good" and "bad" for BAQI is determined assigning the values of the weights calculated according to the opinion of Technical and Practical User-Experts. The values expressed in Table 8.10 plus the corresponding fraction value will be assigned, if the biometric attribute x accomplishes the constraints previously established. The calculation of BAQI has three variations: the first considering just the values of each attribute which accomplish the constraint related, the second considering the value of each attribute plus the relevance obtained for that attribute from Technical User Experts opinion and the third considering the value of each attribute plus the relevance obtained for that attribute from Practical User Experts opinion. Formula (8.15), Formula (8.16) and Formula (8.17) express the calculation of BAQI in its variations.

$$BAQI = \sum_{i=1}^{n} s_i \tag{8.15}$$

Where s_i is the share value of the attribute defined with a value of 0.1250000 and i controls the contribution of every attribute that accomplishes the related constraint.

$$BAQI(TUE) = \sum_{i=1}^{n} W_i(TUE) \tag{8.16}$$

Where $W_i(TUE)$ is the weight of the attribute defined in Formula 8.7 applying the relevance assigned by the Technical User Experts and i controls the contribution of every attribute. The calculus for BAQI(PUE) expressed in Formula 8.17 has the variation of $W_i(PUE)$ which is the weight of the attribute defined in Formula 8.8 applying the relevance assigned by the Practical User Experts and i controls the contribution of every attribute that accomplishes the related constraint.

$$BAQI(PUE) = \sum_{i=1}^{n} W_i(PUE) \tag{8.17}$$

Table 8.10: Parameters to Calculate the Biometric Attribute Quality Index

Attribute	Constraint	W (TUE)	W (PUE)
Pose Angle	-5<pa>5 degrees	0.0648148	0.0833334
Width of head	Wh/Wi > 5/7 minimum 180 pixels	0.0879630	0.0925926
Length of head	> 80%	0.0879630	0.0601851
Horizontally cen-tered face	Cex = Wi/2	0.0833333	0.0972223
Vertical Position	$30\% < \frac{C_{ey}}{H_i<50}\%$	0.0972222	0.0694445
Distance between center of both eyes	$ED \leq 90 pixels$	0.0046296	0.0046296
Resolution	at least 180 pixels of Wh	0.0787037	0.0740741
Number of faces	Only one face is ac-cepted	0.0092593	0.0092593

The highest quality index occurs when all biometric attributes accomplish the constraints. In this case the values obtained for BAQI using the weight of the biometric attributes establishing the reference values for BAQI. A valid value of $BAQI(TUE) = 0.5138889$ and $BAQI(PUE) = 0.4907409$. If the value of BAQI for a desired digital passport photograph results smaller than one of both values, it implies there is missing one or more attributes that did not accomplish the quality requirements.

8.3   Non-Conformance Quality Index

The Non-Conformance Quality Index (NCQI) is based on the fourth Quality's absolute of Philip Crosby's philosophy: *"The measurement of Quality is the price of nonconformance"* [13]. The new quality measurement proposed is based on the representation of the quality information in the minimum unit of information storage: the byte. Where the nonconformance of a quality attribute is stored in a bit, there it is faster and easier to identify depending on it's value and it's position which attribute has or doesn't have quality conformance. For a digital passport photograph the representation of the quality attributes is defined by four bytes. Every byte has eight bits and every bit represents an attribute.

The bytes distribution is as follows:

- *Byte 1 and Byte 2* store the information of photograph quality attributes: Antiquity, image width, image height, Focus, Lighting Scene, Dermis, Background, Eyes, Facing, Head, Percentage, Exposure, Expression, Mouth, No Flash Reflection.

	Antiquity	Image width	Image height	Focus	Lighting	Dermis	Background	Eyes
1	1	1	1	1	1	1	1	1

	Free bit	Facing	Head	Percentage	Exposure	Expression	Mouth	No flash reflection
2	0	1	1	1	1	1	1	1

	Free bit	Brightness	Contrast	Color	Red eye	File type	Blur noise	Impulsive noise
3	0	1	1	1	1	1	1	1

	Head pose angle	Length of head	Width of head	Number of face	Horizontally centered face	Vertical position	Resolution	Eye center
4	1	1	1	1	1	1	1	1

Figure 8.1: Bytes of Non-Conformance Quality Index for a Digital Passport Photograph

- *Byte 3* stores the information of image quality attributes: Brightness, Contrast, Color, Red eye, File type, Blur noise, Impulsive noise.

- *Byte 4* stores the information of biometric quality attributes: Head pose angle, Length of head, Width of head, Number of faces, Horizontally centered face, Vertical position, Resolution, Distance between center of both eyes

Figure 8.1 shows the distribution of attributes in the different bytes.
This group of four bytes is called Non Conformance Quality Index (NCQI). The quality of a facial image in total can be represented by 32 attributes from which 30 are identified, the rest are considered as attributes to be included in the available free bits of the corresponding bytes. In this thesis it is proposed to consider thirty elements adding image width and image height each as one attribute instead of image size; the other two attributes to add are impulsive noise and blur noise.

The NCQI of a perfect facial image is represented by one hexadecimal value for each byte. The quality attributes corresponding to image quality and biometric content are developed in this thesis and they are located in bytes number three and number four, see Figure 8.2. A full conformance of image attributes is represented by 7F in hexadecimal, 01111111 in binary and 127 in decimal; this byte should not have a higher value as 7F. A full conformance of biometric attributes is represented by FF in hexadecimal, the equivalent binary value is 11111111 and 255 in decimal. Byte number three contains seven active bits, byte four contains eight active bits. Depending on the value of a byte it is easier and faster to identify which attribute posseses non-conformance. For example for the value of byte number three it's equivalent number in hexadecimal 1B and in binary is 00011011; in this example it means that the file is not compressed and consequently is a non-conformance attribute. The non-conformance quality index is more precise as it does not accept middle values or levels for an attribute. As default all bits are turned on (having value 1), if an atribute x does not accomplish the conformance expression the correspondent bit is turned off (assigning value zero), if the conformance expression is covered then the bit keeps on. The use of the NCQI depends on the implementation

	Free bit	Brightness	Contrast	Color	Red eye	File type	Blur noise	noise
3	0	1	1	1	1	1	1	1

	Head pose angle	Length of head	Width of head	Number of face	Horizontally centered face	Vertical position	Resolution	Eye center
4	1	1	1	1	1	1	1	1

Figure 8.2: Bytes of the Non-Conformance Quality Index of Image Attributes and Biometric Attributes

of image quality conformance requirements presented in Table 8.7 and in biometric quality conformance requirements located in Table 8.7. If the attribute for a certain photograph covers the conformance requirement, the corresponding bit for the attribute in evaluation keeps value 1, if not, the bit is turned off assigning a zero.

The four bytes proposed in Figure 8.1 can be implemented in the field quality of the Image Information from the face image record format specified of the ISO 19794-5 document[4], as it can be seen in Figure 8.3. Originally the field quality has two bytes and is recommended to be expanded to four bytes according to Figure 8.1. The increment of two more bytes for the field quality can save 8 bytes of the total length of the image data format and 2 bytes of the facial record header as can be visualized in Figure 8.4.

The facial record header can be reduced from 14 to 12 bytes. The two bytes to be eliminated correspond to the position of number of facial images field. Using the NCQI it is not necessary to include the number of facial images as isolated field since it is considered as a conformance requirement to be stored in byte number four of the quality field. Following the logic of the NCQI, if the number of facial images is more than one the corresponding bit is turned off. The facial information field is originally defined in 20 bytes. With the implementation of the NCQI that field can be reduced to 12 bytes. The bytes to be eliminated are related to expression (2 bytes), pose angle (3 bytes), pose angle uncertainty (3 bytes). Expression is an attribute which should be controlled in the acquisition phase and it's validation should be stored in the second byte as proposed in Figure 8.1. The quality of the photograph is assured at the moment of being taken. A validation of the expression can also later be stored in the corresponding bit. Pose angle and pose angle-uncertainty can also be validated and stored in the quality field in the byte number four in the bits corresponding to head pose angle, vertical position and horizontally centered face.

8.4   Validation Protocol

Face images play a significant role as biometric identifier. The accurate authentication of individuals has become more and more important over the years. The passport photograph quality acceptance procedure presently used is based on the human visual perception which is more or less subjective. The quality of an image in general can be automatically calculated by different algorithms, but there is not yet an automated procedure existing for the determination of digital passport photographs quality. This section explains a new developed model to face

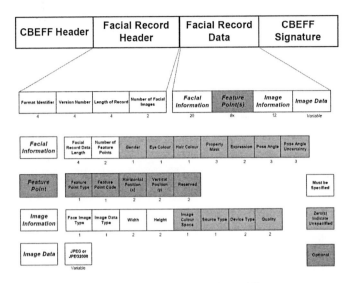

Figure 8.3: Original Face Image Record Format

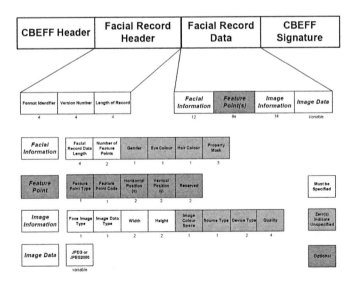

Figure 8.4: Proposed Face Image Record Format

with that challenge.

8.4.1 Objective of the Model

Objective of the model is to determine the quality of a digital passport photograph based on the automated comparison with selected reference values contained in a database. The model could become the base for further developments defining new selected values from a database with different attributes and characteristics. It could find applications in the automated and standardized quality control of digital passport photographs for the expedition of personal identification documents such as visa, passport or driver´s license.

8.4.2 Explanation of the Model

The model presented in this section is based on the interpretation of "good" and "bad" quality. A database containing different values like contrast, brightness, etc. of about fifty facial images was created. These photographs have been taken under very strict and controlled standarized conditions. The database is called "Cualli dataset". The values were obtained considering the requirements defined in the documents ICAO/MRTD [48] and ISO/IEC 19794-5 [4]. The quality of any other photograph can be calculated based on the comparison with the values of the "Cualli dataset".

A node-event diagram represents the workflow of the developed model as shown in Figure 8.5. The model contains five main events represented by main nodes: 1. Validation of catalogs, 2. Photographs evaluation as image, 3. Photograph evaluation as biometric sample, 4. Metrics for the calculation of quality, 5. Passport photograph quality diagnostic. Each event-node has one or more sub-nodes. The relation between events is established through lanes as shown in the diagram. The content of the events and nodes is described in the following list:

1. **Validation of catalogs**

    1.1. File type

    1.2. Attribute

    1.3. Colorspace

    1.4. Quality´s conformance

2. **Photograph evaluation as image**

    2.1. Contrast

    2.2. Brightness

    2.3. Impulsive noise

    2.4. Blur noise

3. **Photograph evaluation as biometric sample**

    3.1. Background identification

3.2. Face region identification

3.3. Eyes region identification

3.4. Mouth region identification

3.5. Nose region identification

3.6. Head region identification

4. Metrics for the calculation of quality

4.1. Conventional quality indexes

4.1.1. PAQI

4.1.2. IAQI

4.1.3. BAQI

4.2. Non-conformance quality index

5. Passport photograph quality diagnostic

5.1. Quality diagnostic

Validation of catalogs. The validation ensures that the input data is correct before feeding the calculation. In the catalog of attributes the considered quality attributes are defined to express the quality of a digital passport photograph. The catalogs should be redefined just if new parameters have to be considered in the calculations, for example: colorspace, grades of quality acceptance or type of file.

Photograph evaluation as image. The evaluation as image returns values for the attributes which define the quality of an image in general such as contrast, brightness, impulsive noise and blur noise are calculated.

Photograph evaluation as biometric sample. The evaluation as biometric sample returns the landmarks of the facial features such as face, eyes, nose, mouth and head.

Metrics for the calculation of quality. The quality defined in the model is calculated with two types of indexes: conventional quality indexes obtained through mathematical methods and the non-conformance quality index which compiles in a hexadecimal value the conformance or non-conformance of quality from the quality attributes defined in the catalog.

Passport photograph quality diagnostic. Finally the determination of the quality acceptance or rejection of a digital passport photograph is determined, a list of attributes which do not accomplish the quality requirements is generated.

8.5 Selected Examples and Results

As mentioned in previous chapters, there are some influence factors which could affect the quality of a digital passport photograph. Certain groups of photographs were measured considering the quality attributes calculated in this thesis. The indexes produced to measure the quality of digital passport photographs are tested using different resources such as the AR

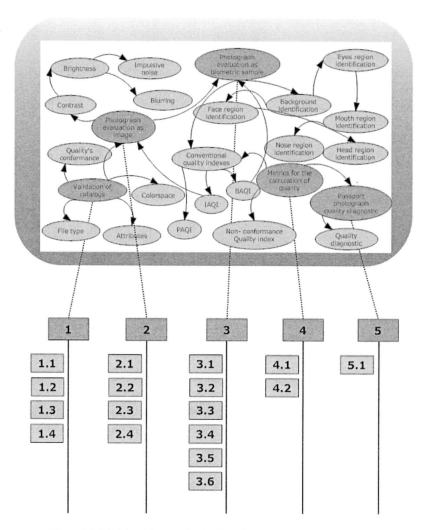

Figure 8.5: Model to Measure the Quality of Digital Passport Photographs

Figure 8.6: Example 1: Photograph $X1$

Table 8.11: Example 1: Values of Photograph Quality Attributes of Photograph $X1$

Attribute	Constraint	Calculated Value
Image width	$W \geq 240 pixels$	413
Image height	$H \geq 320 pixels$	531
Background identifiable	0 if there was no segmentation	1

database [2], *Cualli data set*, FERET database [34] and images of a database created specially for this thesis.

The evaluation of the quality metrics defined for Image Quality Attributes (IQA) is applied to an evaluated photograph named $X1$ shown in Figure 8.6. The photograph quality attributes' values of photograph $X1$ are presented in Table 8.11.

As can be seen in Table 8.11, all the retrieved values of photograph $X1$ accomplishes the constraints established. After this validation the calculation of values for PAQI, PAQI(TUE) and PAQI(PUE) of photograph $X1$ is expressed as follows:

Using Formula 8.9

$PAQI = \sum_{i=1}^{n}(S_i)$

$PAQI = 0.333333 + 0.333333 + 0.333333$

$PAQI = 1$

Table 8.12: Example 1: Values of Image Quality Attributes of Photograph $X1$

Colorspace	Contrast	Brightness	Impulsive Noise	Blur Noise
CIE Lab D65	0.022022	0.828219	0	$2.8e - 005$
CIE XYZitu D65	0.050936	0.623591	$1.3e - 005$	0.000112
Hue saturation brightness	0.052617	0.620629	$1.4e - 005$	0.000272
Hue saturation lightness	0.051636	0.634478	$1.4e - 005$	0.000258
Hue saturation value	0.040895	0.752074	$1.4e - 005$	0.00052
Normalized RGB	0.054501	0.643421	$1.9e - 005$	$3.6e - 005$

Applying Formula 8.10

$$PAQI(TUE) = \sum_{i=1}^{n}(W_i(TUE))$$

$$PAQI(TUE) = 0.1419753 + 0.1419753 + 0.2962963$$

$$PAQI(TUE) = 0.5802469$$

and with Formula 8.11

$$PAQI(PUE) = \sum_{i=1}^{n}(W_i(PUE))$$

$$PAQI(PUE) = 0.154321 + 0.154321 + 0.234568$$

$$PAQI(PUE) = 0.54321$$

The values of PAQI are *plain*, it means that there is no influence factor that interferes to measure the photograph attributes. This means, that there is just a unique value for each index. In the case of Image Attributes Quality, the values calculated for IAQ Index vary according to the colorspace.
The values for contrast, brightness, blur noise and impulsive noise obtained for the different colorspaces are presented in Table 8.12.

These values are considered to demonstrate the diversity of IAQ values, nevertheless as referred in Chapter 6 the colorspace recommended to use in the calculation of quality metrics for people with caucasian characteristics is the colorspace $CIELabD65$. The following calculations are examples of how the image attribute values should be considered to obtain the image attributes quality index (IAQI). The values for all variations of the index and for all colorspaces are presented in Table 8.13.

Applying Formula 8.12 to calculate IAQI:

$$IAQI = C + B - (IN + BN)$$

$$IAQI(CIEXYZituD65) = 0.050936 + 0.623591 - (1.3e - 005 + 0.000112)$$

$$IAQI(CIEXYZituD65) = 0.6744020$$

Comparing the value obtained for $IAQI(CIEXYZituD65) = 0.6744020$ with the reference values of IAQI and IAQI(T) from Table 8.8 with the reference values of IAQI for compressed files, where $IAQI(CIEXYZD65) = 0.663227$ and $IAQI(T)(CIEXYZD65) = 0.903392$ the result of the value obtained for photograph $X1$ is located in the range of acceptance, then from the Image Attributes Quality Index obtained for this photograph for the colorspace $CIEXYZituD65$ can be qualified as "good".

Applying the values of photograph 03a.jpg to Formula 8.13 to calculate IAQI(TUE):

$$IAQI(TUE) = C \cdot W_C(TUE) + B \cdot W_B(TUE) - (IN + BN) + W_{FT}(TUE)$$

$$IAQI(TUE)(CIEXYZituD65) = 0.050936 \cdot 0.0962963 +$$
$$0.623591 \cdot 0.1185185 - (1.3e - 005 + 0.000112) + 0.0222222$$

$$IAQI(TUE)(CIEXYZituD65) = 0.1009092$$

And for Formula 8.14 to calculate IAQI(PUE):

$$IAQI(PUE) = C \cdot W_C(PUE) + B \cdot W_B(PUE) - (IN + BN) + W_{FT}(PUE)$$

$$IAQI(PUE)(CIEXYZituD65) = 0.050936 \cdot 0.1777778 +$$
$$0.623591 \cdot 0.1925926 - (1.3e - 005 + 0.000112) + 0.0222222$$

$$IAQI(PUE)(CIEXYZituD65) = 0.1512515$$

Both values obtained are within the ranks defined for IAQI(TUE) and IAQI(PUE) in Table 8.8. Table 8.13 shows all the IAQI values obtained for photograph $X1$ for the different colorspaces. The calculated values for biometric quality attributes of photograph $X1$ are presented in Table 8.14.

As can be observed in Table 8.14 all the biometric quality attribute values obtained from photograph $X1$ accomplishes the constraints defined, then the calculation of Biometric Attributes Quality Index (BAQI) in its different variations using for BAQI the Formula 8.15, for BAQI(TUE) the Formula 8.16 and for BAQI(PUE) the Formula 8.17 are expresed as follows:

Table 8.13: Example 1: Image Quality Attributes Indexes of Photograph $X1$

Colorspace	IAQI	IAQI(TUE)	IAQI(PUE)
CIE Lab D65	0.8502130	0.1224741	0.1856181
CIE XYZitu D65	0.6744020	0.1009092	0.1512515
Hue saturation brightness	0.6729600	0.1005590	0.1508189
Hue saturation lightness	0.6858420	0.1021199	0.1533257
Hue saturation value	0.7924350	0.1147609	0.1738023
Normalized RGB	0.6978670	0.1036727	0.1557744

Table 8.14: Example 1: Biometric Quality Attributes Indexes of Photograph $X1$

Attribute	Constraint	Value
Pose angle	-5<pa>5 degrees	0.440728
Width of head	Wh/Wi > 5/7 minimum 180 pixels	312
Length of head	> 80%	432
Horizontally centered face	Cex = Wi/2	211
Vertical position	$30\% < \frac{C_{ey}}{H_i < 50}\%$	293
Distance between center of both eyes	$ED \leq 90 pixels$	77
Resolution	at least 180 pixels of Wh	312
Number of faces	Only one face is accepted	1

$BAQI = \sum_{i=1}^{n}(s_i)$

$BAQI = 0.125000 + 0.125000 + 0.125000 + 0.125000+$
$0.125000 + 0.125000 + 0.125000 + 0.125000$

$BAQI = 1$

for BAQI(TUE) the values are calculated with the following data:

$BAQI(TUE) = \sum_{i=1}^{n}(W_i(TUE))$

$BAQI(TUE) = 0.0648148 + 0.0879630 + 0.0879630 + 0.0833333+$
$0.0972222 + 0.0046296 + 0.0787037 + 0.0092593$

$BAQI(TUE) = 0.5138889$

Photograph $X1$ was selected to be analyzed with previous knowledge that it has "good" quality, and as result all indexes' values are perfect. A representation of all values for photograph $X1$ are shown in
and for BAQI(PUE) as follows:
$BAQI(PUE) = \sum_{i=1}^{n}(W_i(PUE))$

$BAQI(PUE) = 0.0833334 + 0.0925926 + 0.0601851 + 0.0972223+$
$0.0694445 + 0.0046296 + 0.0740741 + 0.0092593$

$BAQI(PUE) = 0.4907409$

The Non-Conformance Quality Index (NCQI) is shown in Figure 8.2, for photograph $X1$ the first two bytes are represented in Table 8.16, Bytes 3 and 4 are represented in Table 8.17. In both tables the accomplishment of the three types of quality attributes can be found. As mentioned in section 8.3 it is assumed at the beginning that all attributes have quality conformance if an attribute has non-conformance the corresponding bit is turned off.
The visual results of implementing the metrics are presented in Figure 8.7, the first image correspond to the original photograph, the second corresponds to the skin region detection and the third corresponds to the face features detection. This photograph is an element of the *Cualli dataset*, the "good" quality is evident in the third image where the face features are well marked.

There are two other examples of quality measurement which are selected because of the characteristics of the photographed individuals. The photograph named $X2$ and presented in Figure 8.8 has as particular characteristics the use of piercing and the over maked-up. For a human visual evaluation this photograph can be accepted as "good" but a digital analysis can reject this photograph because the piercing and over make-up affect the identification of facial

Table 8.15: Example 1: Quality Attributes Indexes of Photograph $X1$

Index	Value
PAQI	1
PAQI(TUE)	0.5802469
PAQI(PUE)	0.54321
IAQI	0.8502130
IAQI(TUE)	0.1224741
IAQI(PUE)	0.1856181
BAQI	1
BAQI(TUE)	0.5138889
BAQI(PUE)	0.4907409

Table 8.16: Example 1: Bytes 1 and 2 of Non-Conformance Quality Indexes of Photograph $X1$

Byte 1 Attribute	Value	Byte 2 Attribute	Value
Antiquity	1	Free bit	0
Image width	1	Facing	1
Image height	1	Head	1
Focus	1	Percentage	1
Lighting	1	Exposure	1
Dermis	1	Expression	1
Background	1	Mouth	1
Eyes	1	No flash reflection	1
Dec value	255	Dec value	127

Table 8.17: Example 1: Bytes 3 and 4 of Non-Conformance Quality Indexes of Photograph $X1$

Byte 3 Attribute	Value	Byte 4 Attribute	Value
Free bit	0	Head pose angle	1
Brightness	1	Length of head	1
Contrast	1	Width of head	1
Color	1	Number of face	1
Red eye	1	Horizontally centered face	1
File type	1	Vertical position	1
Blur noise	1	Resolution	1
Impulsive noise	1	Eye center	1
Dec value	127	Dec value	255

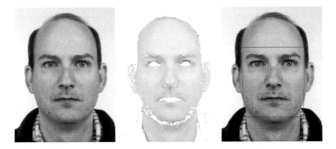

Figure 8.7: Example 1: Visual Results of Photograph $X1$

Table 8.18: Examples 2 and 3: Quality Attributes Indexes of Photograph $X2, X3$

Index	Value of $X2$	Value of $X3$
PAQI	1	1
PAQI(TUE)	0.5802469	0.5802469
PAQI(PUE)	0.54321	0.54321
IAQI	0.7972380	0.8416450
IAQI(TUE)	0.1162550	0.1214989
IAQI(PUE)	0.1754694	0.1840271
BAQI	0.8750000	0.4305556
BAQI(TUE)	0.5092593	0.4120372
BAQI(PUE)	0.9768522	0.4861113

features such as the position of the eyes and the mouth region position. The third image of Figure 8.8 shows the result of facial features identification. The values of the BAQI indexes are shorter than the values obtained for photograph $X1$. The Non-conformance Quality Index expresses as well a shorter value for the byte number four where the center of both eyes is stored. The NCQI for photograph $X2$ is presented in Table 8.20. The third example shown in Figure 8.9, was selected because one of the individual's eyes is looking to another direction not direct to the camera as it is established in the constraints related with the eyes. This problem with that eye has influence in the quality calculation of horizontally centered face and the detection of center of both eyes. The detection of horizontal center of the face is based on the values of center between both eyes and since the horizontal center of both eyes can not be correctly detected for this photograph, the quality indexes didn't take into account both quality attributes. The affected attributes are easy to idenfy in the byte number four. A perfect quality in this fourth byte should have a value of 255, however in the fourth byte of photograph $X3$ its value is 246. The distribution of bytes for photograph $X3$ is presented in Table 8.20. In an extrict interpretaion of the quality constraints photographs $X2$ and $X3$ should be not accepted because they have "bad" quality and their characteristics affect the performance of the software for detection of facial features. The results which support this decision are shown in Figure 8.8 and Figure 8.9.

8.6   Conclusions

The measures proposed in this thesis are results of the measurement of the quantitative and qualitative values of the digital passport photographs' attributes defined in the standards [48] [4]. Atzeni and Lioy in [26] define that a measurement system should exhibit some properties in order to be effective and useful:

Table 8.19: Examples 2 and 3: Bytes 1 and 2 of Non-Conformance Quality Indexes of Photograph $X2, X3$

Byte 1 Attribute	X2	X3	Byte 2 Attribute	X2	X3
Antiquity	1	1	Free bit	0	0
Image width	1	1	Facing	1	1
Image height	1	1	Head	1	1
Focus	1	1	Percentage	1	1
Lighting	1	1	Exposure	1	1
Dermis	1	1	Expression	1	1
Background	1	1	Mouth	1	1
Eyes	1	1	No flash reflection	1	1
Dec value	255	255	Dec value	127	127

Table 8.20: Examples 2 and 3: Bytes 3 and 4 of Non-Conformance Quality Indexes of Photograph $X2, X3$

Byte 3 Attribute	X2	X3	Byte 4 Attribute	X2	X3
Free bit	0	0	Head pose angle	1	1
Brightness	1	1	Length of head	1	1
Contrast	1	1	Width of head	1	1
Color	1	1	Number of face	1	1
Red eye	1	1	Horizontally centered face	1	0
File type	1		1 Vertical position	1	1
Blur noise	1	1	Resolution	1	1
Impulsive noise	1	1	Eye center	0	0
Dec value	127	127	Dec value	254	246

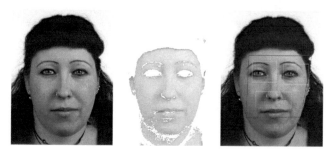

Figure 8.8: Example 2: Visual Results of Photograph $X2$

Figure 8.9: Example 3: Visual Results of Photograph $X3$

- Clarity; A measure should be easy to interpret

- Objectiveness: The measure should not be influenced by the measurer will, or beliefs, or actual feeling

- Repeatability: If repeated in the same context, with exactly the same conditions, the measure should return the same result

- Easiness: The measure of an attribute should raise knowledge about the entity itself, sometimes with the purpose of improving the usefulness of the entity

- Succinctness: Only important parameters should be considered, letting aside aspects not important to the definition and/or the comprehension of the entity under measurement

8.7 Summary of Chapter Quality Metrics for Digital Passport Photographs

In this chapter series of formulae to calculate conventional quality indexes and a non-conformance quality index for a digital passport photograph are created and implemented into the image record format of the ISO 19794-5. The quality of a digital passport photograph is expressed implementing measurements for the image quality attributes and for biometric quality attributes. For conventional metrics there are three different formulae proposed to calculate Photograph Quality Attributes (PAQI), Image Quality Attributes (IAQI) and three possible formulae to calculate Biometric Attributes Quality Index (BAQI). Another form of metric is defined by the Non-Conformance Quality Index (NCQI). The NCQI is represented in four bytes. The four bytes proposed in Figure 8.1 can be implemented in the field Quality of the Image Information from the face image record format specified of the ISO 19794-5 Document [4], as it can be seen in Figure 8.3. Originally the field Quality has two bytes and is recommended to be expanded to four bytes which are defined in Figure 8.1. The increment of two bytes more can save 8 bytes of the total length of the image data format and 2 bytes of the facial record header as can be visualized in Figure 8.4. The attributes considered to be saved on a separated byte can be validated before to be stored and the quality conformance value can be stored in the corresponding bit from one of the new four bytes proposed. NCQI can help the user to assess the quality of a determined conformance requirement defined in the international standards [48], [4] depending on its value and position on a certain byte. The NCQI of a perfect facial image is represented by one hexadecimal value for each byte.

Chapter 9

Conclusions

This thesis describes the development and implementation of different methods to measure the quality of digital passport photographs through a methodology for the abstraction of the quality conformance requirements of the Machine Readable Travel Documents (MRTD) document from the International Civil Aviation Organization (ICAO) ICAO/MRTD [48] and from the document of the International Standardization Organization called Biometric Data Interchange Formats Part Five for Face Image Data (ISO/IEC 19794-5) [4].

Series of formulas to calculate conventional quality indexes and a non-conformance quality index for a digital passport photograph are created and implemented by the author to arise the objective of this thesis. The quality of a digital passport photograph is expressed by implementing measurements for the image quality attributes and for biometric quality attributes.

This chapter grants a conclusion by presenting an overview of contributions, discussion of results and recommendations for future research.

9.1 Summary of Contributions

Different methods to achieve the research objective of this thesis are introduced in Chapter 4. Based on these methods, a methodology called *Achto Cualli* has been created that permits the abstraction of quality conformance requirements to clarify what is the meaning of the quality specified. The methodology contains three matrixes and every matrix comprehends the name of the attribute and the conformance requirement sentence or sentences corresponding to each attribute. The first matrix lists specifications of photograph requirements, the second contains specifications for image requirements and the third lists the biometric requirements identified. The matrixes are useful for a systematic identification of the specified requirements and the constraints that every attribute must accomplish. The specification of conformance requirements may differentiate conformance claims by designating different degrees of acceptance for the evaluation of the requirements validity. In order to indicate the permissibility of requirements extensions a precedence order of evaluation shall be defined for every group of requirements.

The concept *quality* has been analyzed finding different types of quality measurements: objective and subjective. In this thesis the quality metrics proposed are based on both types of quality measurements because they are considered as complement of each other. The found scales to measure the quality describe different types of measurement according the use of the term quality and according the quality requirements specified. As research result it can be inferred that quality is not absolute. There are degrees of quality acceptance and they must be determined by quality managers depending on the degree of quality application and the quality's meaning used. These recommendations suggest that quality can be customized. The concept of Quality this thesis is based on is: *Quality is the degree by which a set of inherent characteristics must comply with the requirements* [24].

The measurement of a digital passport photographs quality in this thesis is developed analyzing the photograph as image and as biometric sample. Image quality is determined by the relevance of the information presented by the image such as contrast, brightness, blur noise and impulsive noise. Most of the presented image quality assessment approaches require an original image as a reference. A quality ground truth or normalizing values or calibration values or quality audit parameters are always necessary to have an indicator for a quality comparison. Some authors of image quality works use an original image as reference. Following this approach has the advantage that one can know the differences between both images. It is not hard to estimate the quality of two similar images having a reference image obtaining approaches of quality with a better exactitude. For digital passport photographs the only normalizing values are the conformance sentences defined in the international standards related and most of them are not quantifiable. After the analysis of image quality measurements the following premises are obtained:

- Image quality cannot be quantified completely by a single metric

- Several image quality metrics have been developed; their goals are to predict the visible differences between a pair of images

- Quality measurements must be accomplished without reference image

- Until now, there are different algorithms to measure a general image quality, there are not yet special algorithms for digital passport photos

In the analysis and design phase of the attributes' qualification, it was considered as hard to assign a precedence and relevance of attributes of a passport photo. For example it is not easy to determine which attribute is more important: resolution or eyes visibility, or for example head pose angle or lighting. Assigning priorities or precedences arbitrarily for an attribute can influence the results of a quality metric. An international survey was designed, to ask experts from Germany and other countries about their opinion and perception of quality, face image quality perception and the use of both international standards. Two kinds of user-experts were surveyed: *practical user-experts* and *technical user-experts*. In the first group people were included whose main work activities are one or more of the following: control, testing, inspection, certification of identity documents with a face image like passport, visa, driver's license etc. In the second group people were included who are related with research in the fields of digital face images, biometrics, standardization, face recognition, passport photos evaluation, IT security, software development, etc. The framework of this survey consists of the analysis of results of two basic frames. The first frame is compound of practical user-experts and the second frame is compound of technical user-experts. These frames are characterized by the use of facial images in the daily activities of both groups of user-experts. The survey was executed in two forms: on-line and on-site. For the on-line survey a web-based application in a three-layer platform (web and applications server, database server, and a web-browser as client) was created. The technical user-experts group was surveyed through an on-line research strategy using different data sources to obtain the email addresses and professional profiles. The practical user-experts group was surveyed through questionnaires applied on-site. In sum 400 experts from 25 countries were invited to participate, 30 practical user-experts and 370 technical user-experts. Detailed results and methodology are described in Chapter 5.

Selected results obtained from the survey refer to: Definition of quality in a general sense, definition of a face image quality concept, relationship between security and face image control, coincidences of user-experts opinions with the requirements specified in ICAO-MRTD and ISO 19794-5 [48], [4], precedence order of quality attributes, relevance order of quality attributes, identification of facial image working groups around the world and opinion convergences and divergences between practical and technical user-experts. The survey is exploratory and it is also used to discover and raise new possibilities and dimensions of the population of interest. The results were published for the face recognition community and found remarkable acceptance, for detailed information see http://www.face-rec. org/interestingpapers/Standards/2dfiqsurveyreport_OYGC.pdf.

Since this survey is an exploratory work, it can be used as the basis for developing concepts and methods for more detailed surveys related to the fields of facial image quality.

A facial image database according to conformance requirements was created and analyzed implementing a methodology called *Achto Pohua* which was developed to find a quality metric for facial images. This methodology was created after the identification of different processes concerned with the development of series of methods to identify, process, and assess the image quality of biometric samples, in this case facial images. The procedures that compound the methodology are described identifying the ingoing and outgoing data. These data permit an overview of the results to be produced implementing the methodology. These results are:

- Metrics for image quality attributes (contrast, brightness, blur noise, impulsive noise)

- Calibration values for image quality attributes

- Metrics for biometric content (head pose angle, width of head, length of head, number of faces, horizontally centered face, vertical position, resolution, distance between center of both eyes)

- Calibration values for biometric content

- Quality metrics for digital passport photographs

- Recommended scenario for acquisition of a facial image database according to conformance requirements

- Usefulness of the Design of Experiments (DoE) technique for analysis of a facial image database

- Identification of skin color influence in the analysis of face image

- Identification of colorspace influence in the analysis of face image

- Anthropometric differences between people from different ethnic groups

A new formula that determines an optimal value for attributes is created as other result of the implementation of the *Achto Pohua* methodology. This formula determines the optimal value obtained for an attribute and it varies according to the values of a dataset from the database according to conformance requirements. It can be expected, that the values of an attribute of a facial image that can be considered as "good" must be between the value of the new variable calculated and the value of the arithmetic mean of the whole data set. This permits to know as how "good" or how "bad" the calculated value should be considered. This new formula is tested using a data set from the quality conformance database and using different data sets. The test results of this new formula are organized according to type of file, attribute and colorspace.

Different algorithms for face and features detection were implemented to test the performance and the compatibility with the results produced in the phase of image quality analysis. The influence of facial image features like hair, shadows, beard and the contour of face is detected. They have an irregular closed curve which does not help to measure the attributes of the features. A method based on the skin color model and an edge detecting based method achieve the face detection and feature extraction. The gray-level threshold method helps to find the background region, while the active contour model method was given up considering the computing speed and the efficiency. Edge detection results can be used to localize the exact position of eyes and mouth. The selected methods for face detection used in this thesis are:

1. Gray-level threshold

2. Skin color mode-based

3. Edge detecting-based

4. Active contour model(snake)

A combination of those algorithms was used to detect the face features. The ground truth of the biometric content of a facial image is determined for an interval of values specified in the standard ISO 197945 [4].
The biometric content attributes identified that can be evaluated are head pose angle, width of head, length of head, number of faces, horizontally centered face, vertical position of the face, resolution of the head and eyes center. The conformance attributes and the mathematical expressions of the features restrictions are constraints or conformance conditions. These mathematical expressions are considered as the calibrating values for biometric content.
The calculi of three quality indexes one for photograph quality attributes (as image width, image height and identification of background), other for image quality attributes (as contrast,

brightness, impulsive noise and blur noise) and the last one for biometric attributes (as head pose angle, width of head, length of head, number of faces, horizontally centered face, vertical position, resolution, distance between center of both eyes) are explained in Chapter 8. The first indexes produced are results of a dataset from the database according to conformance requirements which are interpreted as the calibration values for digital passport photographs for people with Caucasian characteristics.

The Photograph Attributes Quality Index (PAQI) is integrated by the cumulative addition of the weights plus the corresponding fraction value of the measured photograph quality attributes such as: image width, image height and identification of background. The Image Attributes Quality Index (IAQI) is defined by the addition of contrast and brightness values subtracting the addition of impulsive noise and blur noise. Noise and blur noise are deviations of a signal away from its "true" value [23] and any value obtained from their addition should be subtracted from the result of the addition of contrast and brightness to warrant an index with "true" values of the signals. The values of datasets image quality attributes from the database according to conformance requirements were calculated for different color spaces and kind of files (compressed or uncompressed). The value of IAQI indicates how "good" or how "bad" the image attributes of an evaluated facial image are.

The measurement of quality must reflect the grade of acceptance of a digital passport photograph and in Chapter 8 the method to calculate the different quality metrics is explained in a glance with the validation protocol. A detailed example of these calculi is described in Chapter 8 using a photograph estimated with "good" quality, other two examples with "bad" quality are described showing the results obtained for each quality index.

The Biometric Attributes Quality Index (BAQI) represents values from attributes specified in the international standards [48], [4]. The *Achto Pohua* methodology was implemented in Chapter 7 to determine the quality of the biometric content. The result obtained is a constrained ground truth which must be accomplished by the measurement of facial image's geometric information such as head pose angle, width and length of head, number of faces, horizontally centered face, vertical position and resolution.

The BAQI must express a value that indicates how "good" or how "bad" the biometric attributes of an evaluated facial image are. The concept "good" and "bad" for BAQI is determined assigning the values of the weights calculated according to the opinion of Technical and Practical User-Experts. The values expressed in Table 8.10 plus the corresponding fraction value will be assigned, if the biometric attribute x accomplishes the constraints previously established. The calculation of BAQI has three variations: the first considering just the values of each attribute which accomplish the constraint related, the second considering the value of each attribute plus the relevance obtained for that attribute from Technical User Experts opinion and the third considering the value of each attribute plus the relevance obtained for that attribute from Practical User Experts opinion. Formula (8.15), Formula (8.16) and Formula (8.17) express the calculation of BAQI in its different variations.

The facial record header specified in the document [4] can be reduced from 14 to 12 bytes. The information corresponding to the number of facial images can be obsolete if the NCQI is implemented, since it is already included in the bit number five of the fourth byte of the NCQI.

When using the NCQI is not necessary to include the number of facial images as isolated field since it is considered as a conformance requirement to be stored in byte number four of the Quality field. Following the logic of the NCQI, if there is more than one facial images, the corresponding bit is turned off. The facial information field originally is defined in 20 bytes. With the implementation of the NCQI this field can be reduced to 12 bytes. The bytes to be eliminated are related to expression (2 bytes), pose angle (3 bytes), pose angle uncertainty (3 bytes). Expression is an attribute which should be controlled in the acquisition phase and it's validation should be stored in the second byte as proposed. The quality of the photograph is assured at the moment of being taken. A validation of the expression can also later be stored in the corresponding bit. Pose angle and pose angle uncertainty can also be validated and stored in the Quality field in the byte number four in the bits corresponding to head pose angle, vertical position and horizontally centered face.

9.2   Recommendations

The quality metrics for digital passport photographs proposed in this thesis are tested and valid for digital passport photographs of people with Caucasian characteristics. In case that further research activities are planned to develop a world wide metric for all races, it is highly recommended to use this thesis as basis to reconstruct the work flow.

The anthropometric evaluation with the identification of *landmark* points, for each race is also highly recommended. These landmarks can help to detect face features of people from different races. A total of 132 measurements on the face and head are documented. Some measurements are *paired*, when there is a corresponding measurement on the left and right side of the face.

The attributes evaluated and used in this thesis are only some from the total detected. The implementation of other algorithms for other attributes can offer a more complete quality metric. The attributes detected from the quality conformance requirements should be evaluated according to their order of precedence. An international authority should assign this order of precedence to standardize the measuring of the quality attributes.

Bibliography

[1] ABDOU, I. E., AND DUSAUSSOY, N. J. Survey of image quality measurements. In *ACM '86: Proceedings of 1986 ACM Fall joint computer conference* (Los Alamitos, CA, USA, 1986), IEEE Computer Society Press, pp. 71–78.

[2] A.M. MARTINEZ, R. B. The ar face database, cvc tech. report #24. Tech. rep., Purdue University, June 1998.

[3] ANTONY, J. "making your industrial experiments successful - some useful tips to industrial engineers". Tech. rep., Quality & Reliability International Manufacturing Centre, University of Warwick, 2005. date of consultation: 17.05.2005 3:30 hrs. Frankfurt time.

[4] BIOMETRICS, I. F. 19794-5 final draft — biometric data interchange formats – part 5: Face image data, 2005. -file-.

[5] BLAIR, T. Minimum common standards for national identity cards. latest consult 20/12/2005.

[6] BSI. A brief history of bs en iso 9000 2000. http://www.bsi-global.com.

[7] CHARMAINE DM ROYAL, G. M. D. Changing the paradigm from 'race' to human genome variation. *Nature Genetics 36*, 11 (2004), S5–S7.

[8] COMMISSION, E. New, secure biometric passports in the eu, strengthen security and data protection and facilitates traveling. Tech. rep., European Commission, June 2006.

[9] COMPANY, H. M. *The American Heritage Dictionary of English Language*, fourth ed. Houghton Mifflin Company, Berkeley Street Boston, Massachusetts 02116, 2000.

[10] CONSORTIUM, T. F. S. T. Image defect metrics, image quality and usability assurance: Phase i project, version 1.0.1. Tech. rep., The Financial Services Technology Consortium, August 2004. http://www.fstc.org/projects/docs/IQUFinalReport2005-12-16.pdf.

[11] COX, I. J., GHOSN, J., AND YIANILOS, P. N. Feature-based face recognition using mixture-distance. In *Proceedings IEEE Conference on Computer Vision and Pattern Recognition (CVPR)* (1996), pp. 209–216.

[12] CROSBY, P. B. The puzzlement of quality. Tech. rep., Philip Crosby Associates II, Inc., September 1982.

[13] CROSBY, P. B. The practical approach to quality management. Tech. rep., Philip Crosby Associates II, Inc., July 1988.

[14] DECARLO, D., METAXAS, D., AND STONE, M. An anthropometric face model using variational techniques. In *SIGGRAPH '98: Proceedings of the 25th annual conference on computer graphics and interactive techniques* (New York, NY, USA, 1998), ACM Press, pp. 67–74.

[15] DO-HUN KIM, HYUN-CHUL DO, S.-I. C. Preferred skin color reproduction based on adaptive affine transform. In *Consumer Electronics, IEEE Transactions on* (2005), IEEE, pp. 191–197.

[16] DRUCKEREI, B. "security features of the passport data page". Tech. rep., Bundes Druckerei Germany, 2007.

[17] DUANE, M. B. Biometrics 101, version 3.1. Tech. rep., Federal Bureau of Investigation, March 2004.

[18] EDWARDS, A. Human genetic diversity: Lewontin's fallacy. *BioEssays 25*, 8 (2003), 798–801.

[19] ERIK HJELMÅS, B. K. L. Face detection: A survey. *Computer Vision and Image Understanding 83*, 3 (2001), 236–274.

[20] ET. AL., J. W. *"Biometric Systems" Technology, Design and Performance Evaluation*. Springer, 2005.

[21] EUROPEAN COMMISSION, J., AND COUNCIL, H. A. 2588th council meeting. Tech. rep., European Commission, Justice and Home Affairs Council, June 2004.

[22] EUROPEAN COMMISSION, J. R. C. Biometrics at the frontiers: Assessing the impact on society. Tech. rep., European Parliament Committee on Citizen's Freedoms and Rights, Justice and Home Affairs, March 2004.

[23] FISHER, R. E. A. *Dictionary of Computer Vision and Image Processing*. John Wiley & Sons, Chichester, New York, 2005.

[24] FOR STANDARDIZATION, I. O. Quality management systems. Tech. rep., ISO, 2000. -file-.

[25] FOR STANDARDIZATION, I. O. *Identification cards – Physical characteristics*, 2003. -file-.

[26] GOLLMANN DIETER, FABIO MASSACCI, A. Y. *Quality of Protection Security Measurements and Metrics*. Springer, 2006.

[27] GUERRERO, J. M. Mögliche konzepte zur bestimmung gewisser teilaspekte einer qualitätsmetrik für passbilder, bericht version 6., 2005.

[28] HAN, Q. Research report on content-based for 2dfiq (two dimensional facial image quality), 2006.

[29] HECHT, E. *Optik*, 3. korrigierter nachdruck ed., vol. 3. Addison Wesley (Deutschland) GmbH, 1991.

[30] HOSKINS, D., TURBAN, R. C., AND COLBOURN, C. J. Experimental designs in software engineering: d-optimal designs and covering arrays. In *WISER '04: Proceedings of the 2004 ACM workshop on Interdisciplinary software engineering research* (New York, NY, USA, 2004), ACM Press, pp. 55–66.

[31] INFORMATION, OF DIRECTORATE GENERAL FOR ENERGY, C. U., AND TRANSPORT, E. C. Driving licenses: ensuring security, safety and free movement. latest consult 20/12/2005.

[32] JABLONSKI NINA, C. G. The evolution of human skin coloration. *Journal of Human Evolution 39* (2000), 57–106.

[33] JAIN, A., HONG, L., AND PANKANTI, S. Biometric identification. *Commun. ACM 43*, 2 (2000), 90–98.

[34] JANET, S., AND COL. Feret - color feret, facial image database. Tech. rep., Image Group, Information Access Division, ITL, National Institute of Standards and Technology, oct 2003. http://www.nist.gov/humanid/colorferet -file-.

[35] JANSSEN, R. *Computational Image Quality*. SPIE Press, Bellingham, Washington, 2001.

[36] KASS, M., WITKIN, A., AND TERZOPOULOS, D. Snakes: Active contour models. *International Journal of Computer Vision* (1988), 321–331.

[37] KEELAN, B. W. *Handbook of Image Quality Characterization and Prediction*. Marcel Dekker, 2002.

[38] LEE, J. Y., AND YOO, S. I. An elliptical boundary modell for skin color detection. In *Proceedings of 2002 International Conference of Image Science, Systems and Technology (CISST '02), Las Vegas, USA, June 2002* (2002).

[39] LIN, T., SHIH, W., AND HO, W. Y. 3d face authentication by mutual coupled 3d and 2d feature extraction. In *ACM-SE 44: Proceedings of the 44th annual southeast regional conference* (New York, NY, USA, 2006), ACM Press, pp. 423–427.

[40] LIQIANG, W. Enhancing the quality metric of protein microarray image. *Journal of Zhejiang University SCIENCE 12* (2004), 1621–1628.

[41] LOHSE, E. "standards: Heading format for data transmission (a usaai) tutorial". *Commun. ACM 11*, 6 (1968), 441–448.

[42] MACKIEWICH, B. "intracranial boundary detection and radio frequency correction in magnetic resonance images". Master's thesis, "Simon Fraser University, Computer Science Department, Burnaby, B.C.", 8 1995.

[43] MARZILIANO P., D. F. E. A. A no-reference perceptual blur metric. In *Image Processing Proceedings 2002 International Conference* (2002), vol. 3, pp. III–57–III–60.

[44] MILAN SONKA, VACLAV HLAVAC, R. B. *Image Processing, Analysis, and Machine Vision*. International Thomson Publishing, 1999.

[45] MING-HSUAN YANG, N. A. Detecting faces in images: A survey. In *IEEE Transactions on Pattern Analysis and Machine Intelligence (PAMI)* (2002), vol. 24, pp. 34–58.

[46] MORITZ STOERRING, HANS ANDERSEN, E. G. Skin colour detection under changing lighting conditions. In *7th Symposium on Intelligent Robotics Systems, Coimbra, Portugal* (1999), vol. 1, University of Coimbra.

[47] MRTD/NTWG, I. T. . Biometrics deployment of machine readable travel documents, annex d - face image data interchange. Tech. rep., ICAO, May 2004.

[48] MRTD/NTWG, I. T. . Biometrics deployment of machine readable travel documents, version 2.0. Tech. rep., ICAO, May 2004. http://www.icao.int/mrtd/download/documents/Biometrics deployment of Machine Readable Travel Documents.pdf.

[49] NATIONAL SCIENCE & TECHNOLOGY COUNCIL, S. O. B. Biometrics "foundation documents". Tech. rep., National Science & Technology Council, August 2006.

[50] NORMAN B. NILL, B. H. B. Objective image quality measure derived from digital image power spectra. *Optical Engineering* (1992), 813–825.

[51] OF TRADE, D., AND INDUSTRY. The evolution of quality. http://www.businessballs.com/dtiresources/quality_management_history.pdf.

[52] PELI, E. Contrast in complex images. *Journal of Optical Society of America 7*, 10 (1990), 2032–2040.

[53] PHELPS, E. A. Faces and races in the brain. *Nature Neuroscience 4* (2001), 775–776.

[54] PINSONNEAULT, A., AND KRAEMER, K. L. Survey research methodology in management information systems: an assessment. *J. Manage. Inf. Syst. 10*, 2 (1993), 75–105.

[55] R. F. HESS, A. B. U. L. P. Contrast-coding in amblyopia. In *Differences in the neural basis of human amblyopia* (1983), Proc. R. Soc. London, pp. 419–422.

[56] RENATO, B. *Le Razze e i popoli della terra. Caucasoid Subraces*, vol. 1. -, 1954.

[57] ROSENTHAL, D. A. Analyses of selected variables effecting video streamed over ip. *Int. J. Netw. Manag. 14*, 3 (2004), 193–211.

[58] RUSSELL STUART, N. P. *Artificial Intelligence a Modern Approach.* Prentice Hall, 1995.

[59] SCIENCE, N., AND ON BIOMETRICS, T. C. S. Frequently asked questions. Tech. rep., National Science and Technology Council Subcomittee on Biometrics, 2005.

[60] SERVICE, U. K. P. History of passports, early days. latest consult 12/12/2005.

[61] SMITH, E. H. B. Bilevel image degradations: Effects and estimation. In *Symposium on Document Image Understanding Technology* (April 2001), pp. 49–55. Columbia, MD.

[62] SOPHIE LIU XIAO FAN, Z. M., AND SAMUR, R. Edge based region growing: a new image segmentation method. In *VRCAI '04: Proceedings of the 2004 ACM SIGGRAPH international conference on Virtual Reality continuum and its applications in industry* (New York, NY, USA, 2004), ACM Press, pp. 302–305.

[63] STAN LI, A. J. *Handbook of Face Recognition*, 1st ed. Springer, 2004. -file-.

[64] SUMNER, M. Office automation: Organizational learning and technological change. *ACM SIGOA Newsletter 5*, 1-2 (1984), 88–95.

[65] TAPSCOTT, D. *The Digital Economy.* McGraw-Hill Interamericana, 1997.

[66] UNION, I. C. Recommendation itu-r bt.500-11 methodology for the subjective assessment of the quality of television pictures. Tech. rep., International Communicatins Union, jun 2002. latest consult 14/05/2007.

[67] VIKRAM CHALANA, WENDY COSTA, Y. K. Integrating region growing and edge detection using regularization. *In Proceddings of the SPIE conference on Medical Image. SPIE* (1995).

[68] WIERSBA, R. K. The role of information retrieval in the second computer revolution. In *SIGIR '79: Proceedings of the 2nd annual international ACM SIGIR conference on Information storage and retrieval* (New York, NY, USA, 1979), ACM Press, pp. 52–58.

[69] WONG A.K.C., S. P. A gray-level threshold selection method based on maximum entropy principle. In *Systems, Man and Cybernetics, IEEE Transactions on* (1989), vol. 19, IEEE, pp. 886–871.

[70] YI-CHIN HUANG, YI SHING TUNG, J. C. C., WANG, S. W., AND WU, J. L. An adaptive edge detection based colorization algorithm and its applications. In *MULTIMEDIA '05: Proceedings of the 13th annual ACM international conference on Multimedia* (New York, NY, USA, 2005), ACM Press, pp. 351–354.

[71] YUN, Y. W. The '123' of biometric technology. Tech. rep., Biometrics Working Group of Security and Privacy Standards Technical Committee, 2003.

[72] ZADEH, L. The concept of a generalized constraint - a bridge from natural languages to mathematics. In *Fuzzy Information Processing Society, 2005. NAFIPS 2005. Annual Meeting of the North American* (2005), NAFIP, pp. 1–6.

[73] ZHOU WANG, BOVIK, A. A universal image quality index. In *Signal Processing Letters, IEEE* (March 2002), vol. 9, IEEE Press, pp. 81–84.

[74] ZHOU WANG, SHEIKH H.R., B. A. No-reference perceptual quality assessment of jpeg compressed images. In *Image Processing. 2002. Proceedings 2002 International Conference on* (2002), vol. 1, IEEE Press, pp. I–477–I–480.

[75] ZHOU WANG, E. A. Image quality assessment: from error visibility to structural similarity. In *Signal Processing Letters, IEEE* (April 2004), vol. 13, IEEE Press, pp. 600–612.

[76] ZHOU WANG, E. A. Video quality assessment based on structural distortion measurement. In *Signal Processing: Image Communication, special issue on "Objective Video Quality Metrics"* (Feb 2004), vol. 9, Elsevier Press, pp. 121–132.

[77] ZHOU WANG, E. A. Why is image quality assessment so difficult? In *Acoustics, Speech, and Signal Processing, 2002. Proceedings. (ICASSP '02) IEEE International* (2004), vol. 4, IEEE Press, pp. IV–3313–IV–3316.

Appendix A

Glossary

Achto Cualli Achto means firstly, Cualli means the best, in Nahuatl an ancient mexican language. The whole meaning is: firstly the best. Achto Cualli is a self-developed method for a systematic extraction of the information that describes the purpose and scope of a conformance clause and the associated issues that a conformance clause shall or may address.

Achto Pohua Achto means firstly, Pohua means to count in Nahuatl an ancient mexican language. The whole meaning is: firstly counting. Achto Pohua is a Self-developed methodology that proposes a hybrid model solution to determine the quality of digital passport photos.

Balloon Energy An adaptive balloon force that varies inversely proportionally to the image gradient magnitude. The adaptive balloon force is strong in homogeneous regions and weak near object boundaries, edges, and lines.

Biometrics Is a general term used alternatively to describe a characteristic or a process. As characteristic, a biometric is a measurable biological (anatomical and physiological) and behavioral characteristic that can be used for automated recognition. As a process, a biometric is an automated method for recognizing an individual based on measurable biological (anatomical and physiological) and behavioral characteristics.

Biometric Requirement A restriction or condition a biometric attribute should accomplish.

Blur Noise/ Blurring A distortion in an image area where there is a little or no detail, but preserving small structures and contrast at the same time.

Classification The assigment of data to groups within a system of categories distinguished by specified parameters.

Conformance Sentence Requirement Phrases, a phrase that describes the accomplishment of quality requirements.

Continuity Energy An energy signal of an image area.

Compression Reduction of the storage space space required for data by changing its format.

Eigenface An early example of employing eigenvectors in face recognition was done by Kohonen in which a simple neural network is demonstrated to perform face recognition for aligned and normalized face images. The neural network computes a face description by approximating the eigenvectors of the image's autocorrelation matrix. These eigenvectors are later known as Eigenfaces.

ePassort Electronic Passport including Biometric Data.

Experiment A test under controlled conditions that is made to demonstrate a known truth, examine the validity of a hypothesis, or determine the efficency of something previously untried.

European Commission Formally the Commission of the European Communities; is the executive body of the European Union. Alongside the European Parliament and the Council of the European Union, it is one of the three main institutions governing the Union.

Face Image Is the mandatory biometric identifier to be included into digital identity documents.

Face Requirements A restriction or condition an image attribute should accomplish.

Facial Image Feature Typical feature within a facial image such as nose, mouth, eyes, chin or crown.

Fraudulent Document Illegal, deceitfully, or trickery document, expended for profit or to gain some unfair or dishonest advantage.

Image Attribute A characteristic ascribed to an image.

Image Requirements A restriction or condition an image attribute should accomplish.

Image Quality The degree a set of inherent characteristics of an image fulfills the requirements established.

Kronecker-Delta A function of two variables, usually integers, which is 1 if they are equal, and 0 otherwise.

Measurable Requirement Considered as requirement capable of being measured, requirement with a previously defined unit, system or standard of measurement.

Metric Quantitative or qualitative value of real world attributes.

Passport A travel document issued by a national government that usually identifies the bearer as a national of the issuing state and requests that the bearer be permitted to enter and pass through other countries.

Passport photograph Face image with specific characteristics such as size, pose of the individual, background and some others. The passport photograph is included in identity documents.

Personal Identity (Document) Document that contains the set of behavioral or personal characteristics by which an individual is recognizable as member of a group.

Photograph Requirement A restriction or condition a photograph attribute should accomplish.

Practical user expert Can be anyone whose daily activities are related to control, testing, inspection and certification of identity documents with a facial image (passport photo).

Quality The degree by series of characteristics comply with the required specifications.

Race A group of persons related by common descent or heredity.

Real World Attribute Is any property of an abstract or concrete existing entity.

Requirement Is some quality or performance demanded of an in accordance with certain fixed regulations.

Sample This concept is used in its different meanings depending on the context. A subset of a population. A biometrics' specimen.

Sobel Edge Detector Is based in the Sobel kernel which is a gradient estimation kernel used for edge detection where the horizontal kernel is the convolution of a smoothing filter.

Technical User-Expert Can be anyone who has experience working with facial images this group of experts include people whose main activities are related to research in facial image standardization, biometrics, face recognition, passport photos evaluation, facial image, IT security.

Teotl Formula Formula that determines the optimal value obtained for an image attribute, it is based in a stochastic calculus.

Appendix B

List of Acronyms

2DFIQ	Two Dimensional Face Image Quality
API	Advanced Programming Interface
AOF	Antiquity
APA	Head pose
BAQI	Biometric Attribute Quality Index
BGD	Background
BMP	Bit MaP
BNS	Brightness
BP	Pitch angle
BR	Roll angle
BY	Yaw angle
CBEFF	Common Biometric Exchange Format Framework
CC	With of Head
CIE Lab	Commission Internationale d'Eclairage (L*, a*, b* color space)
CIE XYZ	Commission Internationale d'Eclairage (X, Y, Z colorspace)
CLR	Color
CQI	Conformance Quality Index
CST	Contrast
DCE	Distance between center of both eyes
DD	Length of head
DIN	Deutsches Institut für Normung

DoE	Design of Experiments
DSCQS	Double Stimulous Continous Quality Scale
e.g.	example given
EBM	Elliptic Boundary Model
EBU	European Broadcasting Union
EXP	Exposure
EXS	Expression
EYS	Eyes
FBI	Federal Bureau of Investigation
FCG	Facing
FERET	the Facial Recognition Technology
FLT	File
FOS	Focus
Fraunhofer IGD	Fraunhofer Institut fur Graphische Datenverarbeitung
GIF	Graphics Interchange Format
HCV	Head
HCF	Horizontally Centered Face
HMM	Hidden Markov Model
HSB	In combination with colorspace for the color value (Hue) (Saturation) Absolute (Brightness)
HSL	In combination with colorspace for the color value (Hue) (Saturation) Relative (Lightness)
HSV	In combination with colorspace for the color value (Hue) (Saturation) Gray (Value)
HVS	Human Visual System
IAQI	Image Attribute Quality Index
ICAO	International Civil Aviation Organisation
ID	Identification number
ID Card	Identification Card
IEC	International Electrotechnical Commission

IP	Internet Protocol
ISO	International Organization for Standardization
ISO 1052	Specifies qualities of hot-rolled steel sheet 3 mm or more thick, flats and bars
ISO 9000	Standard for quality management systems – Fundamentals and vocabulary
ISO/IEC 10918	Standard of information technology – Digital compression and coding of continuous-tone still images: Requirements and guidelines
ISO/IEC 19785	Standard of Information Technology – Common Biometric Exchange Formats Framework – Part 1: Data element specification
ISO/IEC 19794-1	Standard of Information Technology – Biometric data interchange formats – Part 1: Framework
ISO/IEC 19794-2	Standard of Information Technology – Biometric data interchange formats – Part 2: Finger minutiae data
ISO/IEC 19794-5	Standard of Information Technology – Biometric data interchange formats – Part 5: Face image data
ISO/IEC 15444	JPEG2000 Image Coding
IT	Information Technology
ITU	International Telecommunications Union
JPEG(2000)	Joint Expert Professional Graphics
LGS	Lighting Scene
LOH	Length of Head
MAE	Mean Absolute Error
MCD	Mouth
MIME	Multipurpose Internet Mail Extensions
MOS	Mean Opinion Score
MRTD	Machine Readable Travel Documents
MSE	Mean Squared Error
NbEdges	Number of Edges

NFR	No Flash Reflection
NR algorithm	No Reference
NRE	Red eye
NRF	Number of faces
PCA	Principal Component Analyzing
PKI	Public Key Infrastructure
PNG	Portable Network Graphics
PRG	Percentage
PSNR	Peak Signal to Noise Ratio
PUE	Practical User Expert: Person who
RFID	Radio Frequency Identification
RGB	In combination with color space for Rot Green Blue
RMSE	Root Mean Square Error
RSL	Resolution
SKT	Dermis
SNR	Signal to Noise Ratio
SPH	Size
SVM	Support Vector Machine
TotBM	Total Blur Measure
TUE	Technical User Expert
UE	User Expert
US	United States
USA	United States of America
UK	United Kingdom
UV A/B	Ultra Violett Type A / B
VP	Vertical Position
WAH	Width of head
ZC	Zero Crossing
ZGDV	Zentrum für Graphische Daten Verarbeitung

Appendix C

List of Publications

González-Castillo, O.Y., Delac, K.,	A Web Based System to Calculate Quality Metrics for Digital Passport Photographs. Mexican International Conference on Computer Science 2007, September 24th to 28th 2007, Morelia, México
González-Castillo O.Y.,	Report: International Survey about Facial Image Quality, On-line Resource of the Face Recognition Research Community, 12.2006 http://www.face-rec.org/interesting-papers/
González-Castillo, O.Y.,	Measuring the Quality of Passport Photos, Bulletin of NIST Biometric Quality Workshop March 8th to 9th 2006, Gaithersburg, Maryland USA
Han Qi*°, Li Qiong*, Yuridia González°, Niu Xia-mu*	A Hash-based Scheme for the Protection of UsersÍnformation in Biometric Systems, *Information Countermeasure Technique Institute, Harbin Institute of Technology, China; °Fraunhofer IGD, 64283 Darmstadt, Germany; Acta Electronica Sinica (China) 2005, No. 12A 2005
González-Castillo, O.Y., Taxonomy of Security,	Proceedings of the International Conference on Computing, Communications and Control Technologies (CCCT'04), Austin, Texas, USA, August 2004. Volume VI, pp 273-278 ISBN 980-6560-17-5
González-Castillo, O.Y.,	Mejores Prácticas de Seguridad para Negocios Electrónicos en México, Memorias del XIII Congreso Interuniversitario de Electrónica, Computación y Eléctrica del IEEE sección Morelos Abril 2003 México
Torres-Alvarado, I.S., Verma, S.P., Palacios-Berruete, H., Guevara-García, M., González-Castillo, O.Y.	DC_BASE: a database system to manage Nernst distribution coefficients and its application for partial melting modeling. Computers and Geosciences 2003, 29(9), 1191-1198
González-Castillo O.Y., P. Verma Surendra,	Cálculo de coeficientes de distribución para el modelado petrogenético de procesos magmáticos, Actas INAGEQ 1997. Vol. 3 No. 1, P. 73

Appendix D

Curriculum Vitae

Oriana Yuridia González Castillo

orianay.gonzalezc@googlemail.com

Information Technologies Security and Quality Assessment, Facial Image Quality, Homeland Security, Biometrics Deployment of Machine Readable Travel Documents.

D.1 Education

Ph.D. in Informatics	Technische Universität Darmstadt. Darmstadt, Germany	2007
Master in Electronic Commerce	Instituto Tecnológico y de Estudios Superiores de Monterrey, Mexico City, Mexico	2002
Bachelor in Informatics	Instituto Tecnológico de Zacatepec, Zacatepec Morelos, Mexico	1996

D.2 Research Experience

Guest Researcher	Fraunhofer Institute for Computer Graphics (Fraunhofer IGD) Darmstadt, Germany Research on IT Security and Biometrics	2003–2007
Research Assistant	Energy Research Center of the National University of Mexico (CIE UNAM). Temixco Morelos, Mexico Development of a system for calculating and modeling of partial melting in magmatic processes	1996–1997

D.3 Employment

Quality Controler of Information Technology Projects	Presidency of Mexican Republic. Mexico City, Mexico	2001–2003
	Responsible for quality control and validation of information technology projects, main focus IT security projects	
Project Leader for Electronic Business	Maypo Pharmaceuticals. Mexico City, Mexico	1999-2001
	Coordination of the implementation of the electronic business strategy, online sales and business processes integration	
Trainer and Consultant	Oracle de México. Mexico City, Mexico	1998-1999
	Trainer and consultant of Oracle development tools for Oracles customers	
Software Developer	Contacto Serfin. Mexico City, Mexico	1998
	Software developer for the departments of sales and human resources	
Lecturer in Computing	Access Learning Center. Cuernavaca Morelos, Mexico Lecturer of the courses of Introduction to Computing, Text processors, Spreadsheets, Introduction to programming, Introduction to internet, Programming in HTML, Programming in Pascal, Programming in COBOL, Programming in Basic	1996–1997
Lecturer in Computing	Centro de Capacitación Técnica en Computación. Cuernavaca Morelos, Mexico Lecturer of the courses of Introduction to Computing, Text processors, Spreadsheets, Introduction to programming, Introduction to internet, Programming in HTML, Programming in Pascal, Programming in COBOL, Programming in Basic	1995–1996

D.4 Scientific Software

DC_BASE	Ignacio S. Torres-Alvarado, Surendra P. Verma, Hypitia Palacios-Berruete, Mirna Guevara and Oriana Yuridia González-Castillo	2003